Korean Classical Literature

Korean Classical Literature

An anthology

Edited by Chung Chong-wha

LONDON AND NEW YORK

First published 1989 by Kegan Paul International Limited

2 Park Square, Milton Park, Abingdon, Oxon OX14 4RN
711 Third Avenue, New York, NY 10017, USA

Routledge is an imprint of the Taylor & Francis Group,
an informa business

First issued in paperback 2016

Korean Culture Series: edited by Chung Chong-wha
ISBN 978-1-138-97409-8 (pbk)
ISBN 978-0-7103-0279-3 (hbk)

Contents

The Korean Classical Fiction and the Romance

CHUNG CHONG-WHA

The Novel and the Romance

One may divide the development of the Western narrative literature into several different stages, using several different names for each of them; the epic covers more or less the whole body of oral narrative and the period up to the time the romance started to absorb entertaining stories of marvellous heroic exploits into prose form. The novel began to emerge in the 18th century when people felt weary of the narrative tradition which was becoming too idealistic and too removed from the reality of daily life. The romance itself in its origin expressed a wish to accommodate the demands of ordinary people and the ordinary world and to break away from the unrealistic pose of the epic when it had moved to the lofty world of poetry and the dreamland of heroic past. When poetry and prose went their separate ways and the epic went further into the mythic world of gods and demi-gods, the romance took the direction of the human world of legends and fairy tales and adopted the clothes of daily prose language. The road from the epic to the romance was a steady descent from the heavens and the top of Mount Olympus to the fairy land of palaces, a steady descent from gods to heroic kings and chivalrous generals. The descending movement of this narrative tradition took a step further down into the world of human beings, ordinary human beings, when the novel came into being in the 18th century in the hands of Fielding, Richardson and Defoe. The fall from gods to kings and then to prostitutes, foundlings and shipwrecked sailors was long and steep.

This constant descent undertook a further fall in the rise of modernism in the early part of the 20th century when writers wanted to explore the dark caves of the human unconscious. They were not content with the realism of the surface of daily life, which formed the basis of Virginia Woolf's famous attack on Arnold Bennet, H.G. Wells and John Galsworthy. Balzac, Tolstoy and George Eliot touched on the subtle shades of psychological changes in the mind of the character, but the 19th and early 20th century novelists largely concerned themselves with the linear movements of plots, leaving the unconscious unexplored. The novel, in other words, carried on another major revolution to accommodate new forms of reality after a 200 year happy tradition of portraying various aspects of the known world. It went into the deeper world of the human mind.

Along this descending line are to be defined characteristics of the novel. First of all, the novel is, in spite of Ian Watt, not a literary genre which was suddenly invented as something completely new by Fielding and Defoe in the 18th century.[1] The novel was an extension of the romance. The novel, when it was first created, took over all the literary elements from the romance, which in its turn had inherited all the folkish as well as heroic components from myths and legends. The novel is in this sense an amalgam of the romance and the oral literature.

The novel, however, differs from the romance in its conventions and spirit. When the novel was first written, its founding spirit was to reject the idealism of the romance and instead to create stories on the basis of realism. The notion of realism was simple in the beginning. When a widow's sexual appetite was described as stronger than her wifely sorrow, as in the case of Euphesian matron's story, it was supposed to be realistic.[2] The novel was a revolt against the fantastic and often improbable nature of the romance, and therefore its object was to present the real world which the reader could apprehend through his senses. Hence it had to be 'underived, independent, and first-hand',[3] in the sense the terminology of the novel was given, meaning original. This spirit drove the novelists to take their subject matter from the familiar milieu of daily life, while the romance often took its source materials from the derived world of mythological stories of Roman or Greek legends. The novelists took their characters from the plausible world, to make them real; thus Moll Flanders was a thief, Tom Jones a fornicator, and Robinson Crusoe a shipwrecked sailor. Characters no longer represented universal types. Instead of abstract names like Mr. Badman and Miss Beauty, characters got real names and became a particular individual. The novel was in fact distinguished from its predecessor by the amount of attention it accorded to the individualization of its characters and to the detailed presentation of their environment. The particularity of description of milieu is typical of the narrative technique of *Robinson Crusoe* and *Pamela*.

Along with these lines time also became particularized. The novel was also distinguished by realistic time instead of unspecified time in no man's land. Place also became more precise and particular instead of being vague. In other words, the novel dispensed with time immemorial in favour of today, and far-away places in favour of here. By achieving all these, the novel became the most important vehicle of fiction for 'the scientific scrutiny of life' rather than presenting the dream world of ideal possibility and the unreal world of wish fulfillment. The novel became the art of real world, and to create the new art the prose style had to be different from the flowery, imprecise language of the romance. The novel refused to adopt the rhetorical style, it employed precise and direct language.

The new realism of the novel called upon the realistic plot. The novel did not allow chance happenings of various events, unrelated to each other. The present was possibly only in relation to the past. The organism of causality became a very important convention for the newly risen art. The characters and plot were deftly intertwined, and the story telling was presented in an organic form.

In contrast, the romance cuts out a very simple form of narrative literature. In its structure the romance moves along a simple, linear development of stories, beginning with the birth of a hero and ending with his death. There is no complicated plot; the story is mainly the hero's adventures in love affairs or military events. To borrow E.M. Forster's expressions, it is a series of 'and then, and then, etc' without any sophisticated arrangement of causality.[4] Things happen without reasons or causes; events move along by unexplained actions based on chances. This does not cause character development of a hero or heroine. From the beginning to the end, the central character (or secondary people) do not change. If a person is good, he is good all the way through. If he is bad, he is bad to the last moment. They are boringly flat characters, faithfully sticking to one aspect of human nature. This makes characters largely machine-like stylized types, representing the universal and the general, instead of being particular individuals.

Naturally, techniques were simple, too. Because it was simple story-telling and because there were no strong chains of cause and effect, scenes or settings were not dramatized; they were directly presented and this caused 'paucity of representation' in the eyes of Henry James. The author of the story was mainly concerned with telling the events, not with the dramatic effect of each scene. If there were any settings to the events, the author described them in the briefest and the most direct manner. As the result of this, the background of events and the settings of actions were very vague. Often the place was described as if it was in no man's land and even the time was not specifically presented.

This is largely due to the fact that the world of romance was an unreal world; it was often a fantastic and improbable world, almost as if it was in fairy land. As D.H. Lawrence put it, 'it is a world where rain never wets your jacket and gnats never bite your nose and it's always daisy-time.'[5] It is also the world where a man and beast talk to each other and where supernatural phenomena take place. It was a mystical world where the reader's reason had to be suppressed and where the author's imagination fled into all directions unrestrained. So, supernatural beings were invoked and ideal beauty and wish fulfillment were granted; hence most stories had a happy ending. Inevitably, the picture of life presented in the romance was removed from the reality of the actual; it was based on ideal truth. In the world of romance, the evil were always punished and the good were duly rewarded.

The romance presented in this way offers various levels of valuation. At the lowest level it is a marvellous fairy tale, at an entertainment level it is a Gothic horror story, but at the highest level it is a symbolic work of fantasy charged with multi-level moanings, like Kafka's *Metamorphosis*, the famous horses scene in D.H. Lawrence's *The Rainbow*, or the epiphany scene at the Marabar Caves in Forster's *A Passage to India*. Here the romance reveals poetic truth which cannot be easily grasped with the framework of our daily realistic understanding. Here the romance touches on the unknowable truth of the unknowable world, which D.H. Lawrence calls 'the dark god' or the depths of the unconscious.[6]

The Romance and the Korean Classical Fiction

Kim Kitong, a leading scholar in Korean classical literature, has pointed out in his *Survey of Korean Classical Fiction* some characteristics of the Korean romance. (I assume here that the nature of the Western romance has fittingly explained the characteristics of the Korean classical fiction. I maintain that with the publication of *Kum-O Shinhwa* [The New Stories of Kum-O] in the 15th century, Korean romance literature started. However, the book is a collection of short stories written in imitation of the ghost stories of the Tang Dynasty, and it is obviously wrong to apply the nomenclature of the first Korean classical novel to it.)

According to Kim Kitong, the main body of the Korean romance centres around the life story of the protagonist in the form of a biography, starting with his birth and ending with a certain conclusive point in his life, often in the height of his youth.[7] The protagonist is usually the son of an aristocratic family, extremely handsome, clever in his study, good at poetry, loyal to his parents and the king, righteous in his social and political outlook, courageous and victorious in war. He marries a virtuous and most beautiful girl, and he is extremely happy. But his idyllic life is interrupted by an evil opponent. The cliché pattern follows, moving towards the obvious happy ending, with the defeat of the villain (often by the means of supernatural phenomena and miraculous chances) and the hero's ascendency in the social hierarchy. He and his family become happy forever after.[8]

Kim affirms that most Korean classical fictions are modelled on this structure, which can be divided into five sections: the story of the hero's birth, the episode of his marriage, the time of difficulty, the phase of ascendency, and the state of happiness. What Kim seems to suggest is that the Korean classical fiction is invariably molded according to a certain archetypal pattern. It is true that most classical fictions when brought under a close scrutiny disclose more or less the same book, with similar structure and similar characters. The hackneyed creation of characters is well reflected in the pattern of the bad and good forever divided, with no chance of reform in the bad and no prospect of the good renouncing his noble and virtuous nature. The romance writers, in other words, created type characters, making it difficult to distinguish one character from another, one novel from another. Kim Kitong quotes the description of the step-mother from *The Story of Janghwa and Hongryun*:[10]

> In speaking of her appearance, two cheeks were one inch wide apart, her eyes were like protruding bells, her mouth in the shape of a catfish, her hair like pig's fur, her ears as big as totem poles. On top of that, her arms mutilated, her legs twisted, with double hare-lips, which, if cut into pieces, would fill two bowls, and her face pock-marked. It was hard to look her straight in the face. Worst of all, she had such a vicious heart that she never hesitated to injure others.

This is a gross example of stilted characterization, which brings the Korean classical fiction close to the stereotyped method of characterization in the Western romance. Kim Kitong finds that the step-mother in *The Story of Janghwa and Hongryun* does not appear so different from that in *The Story of Kongji and Patji* or in *The Story of Chung Ulsun*.

Along with the stilted way of characterization, the stereotyped description of settings also puts the two close together. Backgrounds are often summarized in the briefest manner or described in such a flowery rhetorical language with heavy reference to Chinese classics and Chinese sceneries that the places referred to fail to arouse a sense of particular locations. Hence the reader is given the impression that he is sent to an unreal world of fantasy land. This is partly due to the fact that quite a lot of classical stories have China for the place of action.

The affinities between Korean classical fiction and the romance abound. In the Korean stories time is not specified or time does not exist; if there is time, it is often very vague, as a result of which the movement of plot is repetetive and slow. Together with sketchy narration of events instead of scenes being dramatized, and together with the unspecified time and the unreal land, the Korean classical fictions, particularly the earlier ones, reveal their strong kinship to the medieval romance. In both the art of narration, the concept of characterization and the theme of story were unsophisticated. Both were often nearer to fairy tales and fables.

However, the sophistication of art, the depth of time, the profundity of characters were gradually attained as both the romance and the Korean classical fiction developed. Since Kim Sisup (1435–1493) wrote the first Korean classical stories, it took another hundred years before a major talent appeared. Huh Kyun (1564–1618) wrote *The Story of Hong Kiltong*, but the book was in its structure and narrative technique not a great step forward from the budding stage of the first classical stories of *Kum-O Shinhwa*. A masterpiece came along when Kim Manjoong (1637–1692) wrote *The Nine Cloud Dreams*. It is a story of love and adventure, on the surface level, full of erotic suggestions and hazardous events. Like a typical romance, the protagonist is handsome, bright, and lucky with beautiful girls; incidents occur one after another (though without climax, which is again typical of the adventure romances) with complications and solutions, and everything ends happily. Suprarational and supernatural means of solving crisis are abundantly employed. The fact that it is a work of aristocratic literature and the background is China also corresponds to the romance pattern with the imaginative world of bygone days. (According to Kim Kitong, all the military romances of Korean classical fiction have China for the setting of action.) Until the rise of the bourgeois romance, the genre was exclusively concerned with the chivalric world of aristocracy, as Northrop Frye classifies the romance into three periods: the chivalric romance of the Middle Ages, the aristocratic romance of the Renaissance, and the bourgeois romance of the 18th century.

The Nine Cloud Dreams, though the author seems to have intended in the major part of the book to allow the maximum amount of carnal and other pleasures to the protagonist in the course of his career as a successful general and politician, has a strong moral and religious message. Yang Soyu, formerly

Monk Songjin, after his worldly success in love affairs and social enterprise, comes to a realization that all the earthly fame and wealth signify nothing but a dream (dream plays a vital role in the whole story), and that the ultimate truth lies in the eternal world of Buddha. Here the author seems to have committed himself to a double theme. The realization of the protagonist's earthly dreams for riches, fame, for his carnal lust for as many wives as eight, and the fulfillment of his wish to build a paradise on earth — this is the first theme the author wishes to convey in the book, and yet, at the very end of the book the author through the use of a dream seems to deny this very first theme and to state in a rather contradictory manner the second theme of pursuing the ideal truth, in the ideal land. This is the same with *The Story of Hong Kiltong*, in which the author, Huh Kyun, made his protagonist achieve his object in this world and yet sent him away to an ideal world. In this sense the Korean romance is Utopian literature.

Kim Kitong affirms that the longing for an ideal world beyond this world is characteristic of the Korean classical fiction. He attributes it to the fact that after the two Chinese invasions, with political turmoil in the central government and corruption in the local governments, life became extremely hard for everybody, resulting in people longing for an ideal world beyond and also seeking consolation in the dream world offered in the classical fictions.

The fact that *The Nine Cloud Dreams* was written originally in the vernacular language of Korean is significant. It echoes the early romance works of the West which were written in the vernacular language of the romance Provençal as against the learned language of Latin, which was the language of religious sermons, theological writings and philosophical treatises. The Korean romance was likewise a pure entertainment for a wider audience, mainly 'ignorant' women readers, catering to the popular taste for erotic and military adventures. Although the first Korean classical story book was written in Chinese and Park Jiwon also wrote his satirical masterpieces in the same language, the majority of the classical fiction was written in the vernacular language of *eunmoon*, largley due to the fact that the learned language of Chinese was officially adopted for the preservation of government records and the system of civil service examinations, as well as the scholarly expression for the high art of poetry. The Korean scholars and politicians of the Confucian school of the Yi Dynasty regarded fiction as pernicious and vulgar and did not allow the lofty language of Chinese to be used for the popular art of entertainment. The Korean classical fiction in this sense has played a very important historical role in cultivating and preserving the native language. And it was very fortunate that Kim Manjoong set an extremely significant example of writing *The Nine Cloud Dreams* and *The Southbound Journey of Mrs. Sa* in the unofficial language of *eunmoon*, the model of which was to be followed by *The Story of Hong Kiltong*, *The Story of Shinchung* and *The Story of Choonhyang*.

The Achievement of the Korean Classical Fiction

While the Korean classical fiction developed and matured, it took two directions. The first course was to the way of the fable and satire, which accorded the nature of the romance. It took the opposite direction of the real world, and it became unreal and fantastic. It also became ideal and moralistic. In search of a utopia, it became critical of the sordid reality of the world and withdrew from human society. In Park Jiwon's 'Huh Saeng Jon' (The Story of Mr. Huh), the protagonist's life is dominated by his desire to keep away from the world. The fact that he spent seven years in his study under the pretence of the preparation for the civil service examination means that he wanted to avoid contact with the real world. When he was finally forced to go into the world and make money, he did so but soon fled to an ideal community which he built on a desert island with thieves, beggars and the poor. When he was called upon to join the government and run the country, he disappeared into thin air renouncing all worldly wealth and power. This makes the whole story a fantasy; Mr. Huh's money making and building an ideal society are all unreal. And yet the fantasy carries a strong message, the message that the success and wealth are ephemeral, and man's true object should be an ideal truth.

Unlike Kim Manjoong, Park Jiwon (1737–1805) does not seem to have any religious message. He does not seek Buddha's guidance, nor Taoist vision. He does not base his view of life on nothingness. In fact, satires and fables seem to be closely concerned with society and the proper codes of decent behaviour and the system of social classes. In the satire of 'Hojil' (The Admonition of the Tiger), the author makes fun of the hypocrisy of a country scholar and a virtuous widow, and in another satire of 'Yangban Jon' (The Story of a *Yangban*), he chides the vulgarity of money and the artificial way of overcoming one's limit. These two stories are the author's deep care for human society and the improvement of its foibles.

Park Jiwon's attack on the wrongs and follies of his society tacitly takes up the standard of idealism against which grotesqueness and anomalies are measured. His idealism and satire explain his use of the medium of Chinese. His stories are closer to intellectual treatise, like the Chinese language stories of 'Hwa Sa' (The History of Flowers) or 'Soosung Ji' (The Annals of *Soosung*), by Imm Je (1549–1587) in which the world of flowers and plants is adopted to represent the human affairs of politics, or in which the nouns and adjectives of human attributes are directly used for the names of characters like Mr. Inweyeji (Gentleness, Righteousness, Good Manners and Wisdom). Park and Imm were both eminent scholars of Chinese classics, and for them Chinese suited their intellectual exercise well.

However, the tradition of parables and satires are not confined to the writings in Chinese. Korean classical fiction was formulated and developed under the heavy influence of Confucianism, Buddhism and Taoism, and is rich with satires, parables and fables. Almost all classical stories are tainted with moral messages, some are strongly religious and some are not. Some are used as vehicles for moral themes in thinly disguised stories, but in some stories, balance was struck and art triumphs. 'Samsulgi' (Record of *Samsul*) is a three volume collection of stories and oral fables, among which 'Three Gentlemen's Recall to Hades by Mistake' (Samsa *Hyung* Ib *Hwangchun* Ki) and 'Three Men's Excursion' (*Samja Wonjong Ki*) are most outstanding pieces of work. The first story has the theme of the impossibility of obtaining happiness like Norman Matson's *Flecker's Magic*, and the second story tells a Korean version of Rip Van Winkle, in which a successful government official visits his friend in the wonderland of a

Taoist Utopia in a mountain. The magistrate of Pyongyang has a pleasant chat with him for half a day, but when he comes home, all his friends and family are dead in the lapse of eighty years.

But these are short stories, and the moral themes dominate too strongly almost at the cost of art. For better works of art with balanced moral messages, one had to go to *The Story of Shimchung* and *The Story of Hingbu and Nolbu*. These are extremely moralistic stories, but unlike 'Samsulgi', or the Chinese stories by Park Jiwon and Imm Je, they are highly entertaining, and they are not theses in fictional form.

It is also significant that both stories were written in the popular language of *eunmoon*, which had a direct access to a wider audience. They are originally *pansori* literature, without a trace of original authorship; they are popular literature for amusement. Yet they are not without deeper meanings. *The Story of Simchung* has for its theme the Confucian filial piety and the mercy of Buddha, and *The Story of Hungbu and Nolbo* praises brotherly love and warns against greed.

Although the punishment of evil and the reward of good is done through supernatural means in both books, there is a sign of emergence of realism. In *The Story of Simchung*, for instance, the blind father expresses the trend for dreams, while the heroine in her heart grasps the realities of her life acting as a more mature person than her father. Simchung certainly represents at least in spirit the impulse for realism, which is carried out in *The Story of Hungbu* and *Nolbu* by a mundane Nolbu as against the principle of idealism in the younger brother.

The spirit of realism becomes stronger with *The Story of Choonhyang*, in which the page boy plays a prominent role whose realistic outlook triumphs in part over the dreamy, idealistic streak of his master. The contrast between the two, though different in structure of the book, is analogous to the opposition at aspects between Sancho and his master in *Don Quixote*.

The emergence of realism in these books foretells a new direction in the tradition of the Korean romance. Technically, *The Story of Choonhyang* is a long way from the realism of the novel, but at least its mental perspective is in the spirit of realism. The fact that there is no supernatural way of solving the problem testifies a new mode of thinking, a new attitude to adjust to the reality of what people accepted and believed.

This means that literature in the 18th century was no longer a high art imposed on people, but a popular form to woo people's patronage, to go closer to them and amuse them. From *The Story of Hungbu and Nolbu* onward through *The Story of Choonhyang*, the element of realism often meant comic scenes and comic views, and indeed a new genre of comedy came into being in the last stage of the Yi Dynasty. *Baebijang Jon* (The Story of Assistant Bae), though the date of composition and the authorship are unknown like almost all Korean classical fictions, is one of the rare literary phenomena in that it tried to accommodate a rather vulgar taste of the low class with its coarse language and its uncouth scenes of laughter. It is an amusing assault on the hypocrisy of the gentry class and on the idle life of the local government officials. However, what makes the book outstanding is that it is a well plotted, and well made work of art. For the first time with this work the Korean classical fiction has definitely moved out of the realm of the romance and set an example toward what one might call the novel proper. The work is written in the vein of satire, but its ironies are subtly hidden in a refined comedy.

Some Problems in the Korean Classical Fiction

A steady attention has been given to the Korean classical fiction and many critical books and essays have been published. But no one has paid any serious attention to the wrong application of the classical novel to the Korean romance. Nor has any critic elaborated on the romance nature of classical fiction. Accordingly a number of errors and problems have been overlooked. Kim Sisup's short stories have been referred to as 'the first Korean novel' or 'the first Korean novel in Chinese'. The same error has been committed to Park Jiwon's short stories, which are still called 'the novel in Chinese'.

A loose understanding of the novel has caused some confusion in the classification of the genre. *Memoirs of a Korean Queen* (*Hanjoong Nok*) is regarded as a 'historical novel'[11] (by Kim Kitong) or a 'court novel'[12] (by Yi Byungki), while the book is evidently anything but the novel; it is a piece of historical record or a plain autobiographical reminiscence by the wife of a crown prince. If *Hanjoong Nok* is a novel, *Sangook Yusa* or *Sangook Saki* can be referred to as a novel.

Why has this misunderstanding of the novel happened? The novel is a direct translation of *sosul*, which by Juantzu and since then meant 'gossips from streets' or 'rumours in town' in the first place and then subsequently any sundry writings other than Confucian classics. When Yi Kyubo first used the word *sosul* in Korea he implied the essay, not the fictional writing; *The Baekwoon Sosul* was a collection of essays on poetry. The novel in the modern sense was a commercial term used by publishers like Yuil Sogwan and Chosun Sogwan around 1913 when a new kind of stories were written in imitation of the Western novel by Yi Injik and other new generation writers of the time. The publishers called the new kind of stories 'the new novel' and the romance stories 'the old novel' or 'the old-time novel', which was eventually refined into 'the classical novel' by Western scholars.

The organic form of the novel with its readiness to incorporate multiple levels of reality and with its own diverse conventions does not apply to the romance. I would like to propose now to call what is the so-called Korean classical novel 'the Korean classical fiction' as I have used it here 'the romance literature of the Yi Dynasty'. At the same time I would like to call reader's attention to the precise nature of the romance, which, extended to the modern novel, has become an important means of exploring the deeper reality of the human heart and the symbolic region of truth. This exploration in the symbolic world beyond our rational experience is what some of the best romance of the Yi Dynasty has achieved.

Notes

1. Ian Watts, *The Rise of the Novel*, Penguin, 1957, p. 7
2. ibid., p. 11
3. ibid., p. 15
4. E.M. Forster, *Aspects of the Novel*, Penguin, 1979, p. 87

5. D.H. Lawrence, *Studies in Classical American Literature*, Mercury Books, 1965, p. 78
6. D.H. Lawrence, *Kangaroo*, Chapter 17
9. Kim Kitong, *Survey of Korean Classical Fiction*, Seoul, 1956, p. 32
8. ibid., p. 34
9. ibid., p. 35
10. ibid., p. 37
11. ibid., p. 143
12. Yi Byung-ki and Back Churl, *A History of Korean Literature*, 1948, p. 165

Park Ji-won
(1737 – 1805)

MOON HI KYUNG

A leading scholar, thinker and writer of eighteenth-century Korea, Park Jiwon is one of the earliest advocates of modernization in Korea, whose thoughts on progress and social reforms inspired by his knowledge of western civilization were to have deep influence on later generations.

Born in a well-to-do scholar-gentleman's family in Seoul, Park Jiwon did not sit for the Senior Civil Service Examination as did most other scholar gentlemen of his days. Instead, he served in various minor posts until he reached the age of 50 when he was finally promoted to a senior post.

He was, however, befriended by prominent scholars and officials who visited China in various capacities and who brought him the knowledge of modernizing China. What perhaps had the greatest influence on his life and thoughts was his visit to China, where he first became acquainted with the western civilization to which the Ching Dynasty had been opening itself up. On his return from China, he wrote his famous *Yul-ha Journal*, in which he made comparative analyses of changing China and static Korea and put forth his ideas on social progress and economic development, strongly recommending China as a model.

In this belief in progress and need for social reforms, Park was not alone. He was one of the leading figures of a new school of philosophy called *Sil-hak*, or Neo-Confucianism (literally studies for pragmatism or realism), which opposed the old Confucianism which had so far dominated all aspects of life in Korea. Criticizing the old doctrine as being too theory-oriented, unrealistic and non-productive, the new school interested itself in more practical and utilitarian aspects, placing emphasis on issues such as the art of governing, development of commerce and skills and techniques and opposition to the rigid feudal class system.

In a sense, the emergence of this new school of thinkers reflected the social reality of the period. Eighteenth-century Korea was a country suffering from many serious and deep-rooted social evils. First the Japanese invasion and then the conflict with China in the previous centuries had left the nation's economy in a state of severe stagnation from which it had yet to recover. Excessive taxation levied on the common people from which the richer land-owning class was exempted, the upperclass monopoly of the land which turned more and more small farmers into mere tenants, and the extreme poverty under which most commoners lived while the rich enjoyed increasing privileges — these and others were evils which set some serious thinkers into reflecting on the causes and means of redressing such injustice.

Of these thinkers, Park is particularly renowned for his ideas on commerce and technology. The basis of his economic theory lies in his belief in trade and technology as means of delivering the commoners from chronic poverty. He claimed that the cause of national poverty lay in the neglect of trade and saw improvements in transportation, roads, housing and even farming tools as essential factors in bringing up the standard of life. For instance, in his tale *Huh-saeng*, through the mouth of his hero, he blames as one of the main causes of the nation's sluggish economic activities the inadequate and slow distribution of commodities, for which a lack of wheeled vehicles and adequate roads were responsible. In his economic theories, Park looked towards the Ching Dynasty of China on whose influence he relied heavily. In this, he differed from most other Confucian scholars who regarded the Ching Dynasty as northern barbarians, preferring to follow the thought and customs of the fallen Ming Dynasty. But, radical as his thoughts must have appeared to his contemporaries, Park can be said to have looked far ahead of his time.

In ethics, too, Park can be said to have been a radical for his age. He opposed medieval authoritarianism and principles of justification and rejected the feudal notion of the class system. He was particularly opposed to the discrimination suffered by illegitimate children and stood up for the common people, insisting on the importance of human dignity and the individual's usefulness in society rather than his birth. *The Tale of a Yangban* is a good example of his satire against the upperclass people called *Yangban.*

These thoughts are reflected in his writings, which, like those of most other Sil-hak scholars, bear a strong imprint of individuality. Though he wrote in Chinese, he insisted that literature should be national and therefore criticized those who excessively imitated the literature of the Han, Ming and Tang Dynasties of China.

Park Jiwon's desire for social reforms did not bear any fruit in his life time. But in his belief in human dignity, in his progressive economic theories, he was without doubt one of the foremost pioneers of modernism in Korea.

‘Hozil’ or The Tiger’s Admonition

PARK JI-WON

The Tiger is gentle and holy, beauteous yet fierce, virtuous and kind-hearted, subtle and swift, strong and ferocious — in other words there is none to equal him on earth.

Yet the *Biwi*[1] devours the Tiger; the *Chukwoo*[2] also devours him as do the *Pak*[3] and the *Five-Coloured Lion*[4] who devours him at the top of the mountain where stands a tall tree. The *Jabaek*[5] also devours the Tiger; and the *Pyogyun*[6] which flies devours both the Tiger and the Leopard; the *Whangyo*[7] devours the hearts of the Tiger and Leopard; the *Whal*[8] willingly lets himself be devoured by the Tiger only to devour in his turn the Tiger’s liver from within; the *Chuwi*[9] tears and devours the Tiger whenever he comes across him; and when the Tiger meets the *Mengyong*,[10] he dares not look him straight in the eye. Yet man does not fear the *Mengyong* but fears the Tiger, by which you can see the Tiger’s bearing to be majestic and awe-inspiring.

When the Tiger eats a dog, he becomes drunk; when he eats a man he performs enchantments. Also when the Tiger eats a man the first time, the spirit of the man comes to be called *Gul-gwak* and attaches itself to the armpit of the Tiger.

[1] Baboon or a kind of monkey.
[2] Literally a Bamboo Cow.
[3] An imaginary animal which resembles a horse. Its body is white and tail black and it has hornlike teeth and claws and is said to eat tigers and leopards.
[4] A multi-coloured animal that looks like a lion.
[5] An animal that looks like a horse but has sharp teeth, which eats tigers and leopards.
[6] A kind of dog which flies and eats tigers and leopards.
[7] A kind of dog which resembles a leopard with yellowish hair on its body and black teeth.
[8] An animal which, when devoured by a tiger, stays alive to gnaw away the inside of the tiger.
[9] A kind of tiger which has a huge body and long tail.
[10] An imaginary animal.

The spirit then lures the Tiger into a kitchen and makes him lick the pot; and should the owner of the house suddenly feel hungry in the middle of the night and ask his wife to prepare him something, he will then eat his second man. The spirit of the second person will then be called *Yi-ol* and cling to the cheekbones of the Tiger. His task will be to observe from a high hill the movements of hunters at work, and should he discover a trap or an arrow buried in a deep valley, he will promptly unlock the trap. When the Tiger eats his third man, the spirit will be called *Yuk-hon* and attach itself to the Tiger's chin. From there, the spirit will constantly call the names of friends that he had known in his life.

One day, the Tiger summoned all the spirits and said to them, 'The sun is near setting. Where shall we find something to feed ourselves on tonight?'

Gul-gwak said to him:

'Upon consulting the stars, I have found that it is a creature that has neither horns nor wings but a black head, and it leaves stumbling footprints on the snow. His tail is attached to the back of his head and he cannot hide his behind.'

Yi-ol now said to him:

'At the East Gate is something to eat and it is called "doctor". In its mouth are herbs of all kinds and its flesh therefore is said to be fragrant. At the West Gate also is something to feed upon and it is called "shaman". It flatters all the spirits and daily washes itself within and without and its flesh therefore is known to be pure. Partake of one of these as your appetite desires.'

The Tiger stroked his beard and frowned.

'Ahm! This "doctor" creature, I know, has taken the lives of tens of thousands of people by trying its uncertain skill on innocent victims. This "shaman" creature also has brought death to several thousands of people by deceiving the spirits and seducing the ignorant people. The curses of these people will have penetrated into the very marrow of their bones and transformed them into *keum-jam*[11], whose flesh is too poisonous to be eaten.'

[11] *Keum-jam*: Southern people bred *keum-jam* whose flesh is known to be extremely poisonous.

Now *Yuk-hon* said to him:

'There is an edible creature that lives in the wood which is known to have a kind heart and a loyal and righteous mind. His integrity is unquestioned and he wears elegance on his head and courtesy on his feet. He can recite all the wise sayings of the sages of old and has mastered the laws of the universe. His name is *Sukduk-chiyu*, meaning a Confucian scholar of great virtue. The flesh on his back is meaty and tender and appetizing beyond anything on earth.'

Only then did the Tiger raise his brows. His mouth watering, he looked up at the sky and smiled.

'I wish to hear more about this creature,' he said.

All the spirits vied with one another to recommend the creature.

'The Divine Principles of Yin and Yang are called the Divine Doctrines, and the scholar has already mastered these. It is said that the Five Elements of the Universe — fire, water, wood, metal and earth — mutually breed each other and the Six Natural Forces — Yin, Yang, Rain, Wind, Darkness and Light — mutually support each other. Since the scholar is said to be able to harmonize all these forces, there would be nothing in the world more tasty and delicious.'

Hearing this, the Tiger's face clouded over and he said in a joyless voice:

'No, Yin and Yang are two inseparable elements which live and die as one. Since they have been divided, their flesh will be impure. As for the Five Elements, they have their fixed places and did not give birth to one another at the beginning. Since they too have been forced apart as mothers and sons, with even saltiness and sourness added to them, their taste too cannot be pure.

'The Six Natural Forces operate by themselves without needing any mutual support. The scholars have absurdly called them *Jaesung* and *Bosang*[12] and falsely given them credit for creating the Divine Doctrines and for establishing the Divine Order. If I were to eat this creature, his flesh is bound to be tough and hard to swallow and will surely give me an indigestion.'

[12] *Jaesung* and *Bosang*: taken from the *Yi-king* (the Book of Changes) of Ancient China.

At about this time, there lived in a village a scholar who pretended not to like worldly fame. His name was Squire Buk-gwak. At the age of forty, he had personally revised as many as ten thousand books and, enlarging upon the Nine Chinese Classics, had written five thousand books, for which Heaven looked down kindly upon him and all the noblemen praised his name.

In the same village in the eastern section also lived a pretty widow called Dongri-ja. Though bereft of her husband at an extremely early age, the widow's chastity was such that Heaven found it commendable and all the noblemen loved her virtue to the extent of calling the village gate 'The Gate of Widow Dongri'. Though thus famed for her chastity, the widow had five sons, all of them with different surnames. One night all five of them gathered outside their mother's room.

'North of the river the cock crows, south of the river the star shines. Dead silence reigns in the room; what is Squire Buk-gwak doing there?'

Chanting these lines, the five took turns to peep into the room. In the room, Dongri-ja was saying to Squire Buk-gwak,

'I have for a long time loved and honoured your virtue, Master. Tonight I would like to hear you read if it pleases you.'

Squire Buk-gwak sat up, arranged his suit and recited a verse:

'"The turtle-doves on the screen, the fire-flies flash by,
Iron cauldrons and three-legged pots, what could they be made after?"
Is it not interesting?'

When the sons saw the scene, they said to each other,

'It has been said that it is a breach of decorum to visit a widow's room. But as Squire Buk-gwak is wise and virtuous, I am sure he is not behaving amiss.'

'I hear that a fox has gnawed its way through the village gate.'

'I have heard that when a fox lives to be a thousand years old, it is reborn and can play at being a man.'

They then consulted each other again.

'I have heard that he who obtains the fox's hat will become the owner of a thousand gold pieces; and he who obtains his shoes will obtain power to hide his shadow in midday; and he who obtains his tail will have power to cajole anyone so that he is welcomed by all. Why don't we kill the fox and divide the spoils among us?'

They surrounded their mother's room and stormed into it.

Taken by surprise, Squire Buk-gwak made away as fast as he could but fearing that he should be recognized, he slung one leg over his shoulder and danced out of the house laughing like a goblin. But as he was running across the field, as ill luck would have it, he fell into a pit. The pit was full of dung.

After floundering for a bit, he at last managed to find a hold and crept out of the pit. Then he looked up. There stood before him blocking his way and growling in no uncertain manner was the Tiger.

The Tiger, his face all crinkled up in distaste and feeling nauseous, held his nose and turned his head away.

'Ugh! How this scholar stinks!'

Squire Buk-gwak, his nose almost touching the ground, crawled on all fours towards him and bowed three times. Then he said:

'Lord Tiger, your virtue is known to the whole world. A wise man learns from you the art of metamorphosis, a king your gait, an adopted son your piety, and a soldier your dignity. Your divine name, together with that of God, raises the wind and stirs the cloud. A servant so humble as myself living in this lowly place dares only to stand at your feet.'

Hearing this, the Tiger admonished him:

'Do not dare approach any nearer. I have heard that scholars are but flatterers and your words prove it true. Considering the impertinent habit you have of endowing the Tiger with all the wicked names on earth, who will be so foolish as to be taken in by your ingratiating words, uttered only because you happen to be in a tight corner now? As there is but one law in this world, when man's nature is evil, so will be the Tiger's nature; when man is gentle, so will be the Tiger. Though the Five Cardinal Virtues are never far from your lips and you preach Four Great Moral Principles constantly, in cities and villages, there are many men whose noses have been cut off, whose feet chopped off and whose faces marked, all for having failed to observe the Cardinal Virtues.

'Yet in spite of this, men are busy making more ropes, more

tattooing needles, axes, saws and such-like instruments and there is no putting an end to their wickedness. But in the House of Tiger, there are no such cruel punishments, by which alone you can see the nature of the Tiger to be more gentle than that of man.

'Also the Tiger does not chew the grass and trees, eats neither insects nor fish; he does not indulge in harmful habits like drinking nor touch such paltry food as roe and pickled fish. He is content to hunt deer in the woods and oxen in the fields and has yet to worry about his living and his daily food. Does this not show the fairness and the brightness of his virtues?

'When the Tiger hunts deer, men do not find fault with him; but when he devours their oxen, men will call him an enemy. This, I presume, is because deer are of little use to men while oxen are useful. Yet forgetting the service the oxen render men by carrying heavy loads and ploughing the fields, forgetting their loyalty and affection for men, is it not true that your butchers' shops are bursting with their meat and not even their horns and skin spared?

'Not content with that, you take deer from us, depriving us of our food in the woods and starve us in the fields, so were Heaven to deal justly with you, should we or should we not in all justice eat you?

'Taking what is not one's own is commonly called thieving; plundering from others and taking their lives sheer vandalism. But regardless of day and night, you men roam about restlessly, your eyes glaring, your sleeves rolled up to take what is not yours with no trace of shame. You have even come to call money your brother and a man has been known to have killed his own wife to further his ambition of becoming a general. Behaving so shamelessly, how could you have the face to talk of moral principles?

'Since you do not scruple to take from grass-hoppers their food, from silkworms their clothes, kill bees and plunder their honey and even steal ant eggs to offer them to your ancestors, what creature on earth could equal you in cruelty and lack of virtue?

'You boast of your faculty to reason and at the slightest need call upon Heaven, but as Heaven has ordained it, both the Tiger and man are but mere animals. The Divine

Benevolence of Heaven and Earth which created and raised all things on earth has decreed that neither tigers nor grass-hoppers, silkworms nor bees, ants nor men shall live in a state of conflict with each other.

'Also, seen in terms of Good and Evil, is not he who brazenly plunders the houses of bees and ants and steals from them the greatest thief on earth? And is not he who indiscriminately steals from silkworms and grass-hoppers the greatest foe to humanity? The Tiger does not eat Leopards because it is not in him to harm his brethren.

'However many deer the Tiger has devoured, its number cannot equal that eaten by men; however many oxen the Tiger has killed, its number also cannot equal that devoured by men. What is more, however many men the Tiger has eaten, it is nothing compared to the number slain by their fellow men. Last year when there was a great drought in Midland in China, several thousands of men were killed and devoured by other men. Before that, there was a great flood in Shandung Province where, again, tens of thousands of men were slain and eaten. But what can equal the extent of fratricide that occured during the civil strife of the Chunchu Era? During that period, seventeen battles were fought in the name of honour and thirty in the name of revenge. The blood stained the fields thousands of miles around and the number of dead amounted to over a million.

'But the House of Tiger is troubled neither by drought nor flood and therefore knows no grievances against Heaven. He knows neither favoritism nor enmity and therefore incurs no one's hatred. He knows and obeys the will of Heaven alone and therefore does not fall under the spell of shamans' or doctors' witchcraft; and living by his nature and obeying the will of Heaven, worldly losses and gains do not touch him. Such are the virtues and piety of the Tiger.

'Moreover, the spots on his back will bear testimony to his intelligence and he does not carry even a tiniest weapon, relying solely on the sharpness and strength of his teeth and claws, which is to display to the world the glory of his arms. His picture painted on dishes with that of the monkey is to proclaim to the whole world his piety, and though he hunts only once during the day, he will share the leftovers with crows and kites and ants. Does not his benevolence, therefore, surpass all description?

'The Tiger does not eat those who tell tales nor does he eat those who are sick or in mourning and his virtuousness and righteousness therefore cannot all be recorded here.

'But the way you find your food is vicious beyond words. Not content with traps and snares, you have made such things as bird nets, deer nets, small fish and big fish nets, wheeled nets and straw nets. The man who first invented the net has rendered a great disservice to the world. On top of that, you have made huge barbs, hand-spears, lances, harpoons, daggers and such other weapons as well as something called the cannon whose very sound, when fired, shakes the mountain to its root and whose fiery flames are enough to unleash the Divinity of Yin and Yang, and whose dreadfulness overpowers that of lightning and thunder.

'But all your wickedness still unexhausted, you have taken the softest of furs and with glue made it into a blade as sharp as a jubjube seed of a length less than an inch and soaked in squid's ink. With that, you slash and pierce as you wish and armed with a triangular blade at the end, it has the keenness of a dagger, the strength of a sword, the shape of a forked spear, the straightness of an arrow and the tautness of a bow. Once this weapon is wielded, all the ghosts are said to burst into loud wails and lamentations at midnight. There can possibly be none who is more cruel and better at devouring each other than your race!'

Squire Buk-gwak got up and prostrated himself anew upon the ground. He got up again and awkwardly bowed to the Tiger again twice, and with his nose to the ground said:

'It is written in Mencius' writings that "however wicked a man is, if he cleanses himself within and without he can become worthy enough to serve the Heavenly King". So your humble servant in this lowly place dares stand at your august feet.'

Not daring to breathe, he lay still waiting for a reply. But no reply came. Feeling apprehensive and overcome with a feeling of great dread, he brought his hands together, bowed low and looked up. The sun was rising in the eastern sky and the Tiger had disappeared into nowhere.

Just at that moment, a farmer who had come to plough the field was passing by and saw him.

'Squire, what has brought you out so early in the morning to make bows to the empty air in this field?' he asked.

'There is an old saying which says, "High though the sky be, how can a man not bend his head low, and firm though the earth be, how can he not tread gently!' murmured Buk-gwak in answer.

translated by Moon Hi Kyung

The Tale of Huh-Saeng

PARK JI-WON

There lived in a village called *Mugjuk* a man named Huh-Saeng. Right at the foot of *Namsan* Hill, past a well was an old gingko tree; a bush-clover gate stood wide open facing the tree and beyond was a small thatch-roofed cottage which but ill kept out the wind and the rain. But Huh-Seng only immersed himself in his studies and he and his wife barely managed to keep alive on what little his wife earned by doing some sewing. One day his wife, unable to bear the hunger any longer, said to him,

'Since you will never even sit for the Civil Service Examination which will get you a position in the government, what is the use of your continuing your studies day and night?'

'Perhaps I have not yet attained a sufficient depth of learning,' Huh replied.

'Then what about becoming a craftsman?'

'Never having learnt the craftsman's art, what is to be done?'

'Then you should at least try your hand at becoming a tradesman,' urged his wife.

'Not having any capital, what is to be done?' Huh replied again.

'It appears to me that all you have learnt from your precious studies is "What is to be done?" If you can neither become a craftsman nor a tradesman, then what about a thief?' retorted his wife now getting angry.

At this, Huh-Saeng reluctantly put away his books and got up.

'Ah! The pity of it! I set out to devote ten years to study but have managed only seven.'

So saying, he left the house but found that he knew no one in town. He went straight to the marketplace and asked the shopkeepers he met, 'Who is the richest man in town?' Upon being told that a certain person by the name of Byun passed as such, Huh-Saeng immediately sought his house. Meeting Byun, Huh-Saeng bowed deeply and said to him,

'There is something that I wish to put to trial. But since I am a poor man, I have come to borrow from you ten thousand pieces of gold.'

'As you wish,' said Byun, promptly handing him the gold. Huh-Saeng, without a word of thanks, took the gold and disappeared out of the house.

Now, to Byun's children and guests in the house, Huh-Saeng looked no more than a beggar. His belt, though girded around his waist, was frayed; his shoes, though made of leather, had the heels worn through; his top hat was battered to bits and his tunic was black with grime. What was worse, from his nose ran a clear stream in an unceasing flow.

After Huh-Saeng had left the house, Byun's children, greatly astonished by their father's action, asked him,

'Father, do you know that person well?'

'I have never met him.'

'Then how is it that you have just lent an immense sum of money to a stranger without even asking his name?' they asked.

'It is not for you to know,' Byun replied. 'Generally, when a man comes to beg something of someone, he tries to make himself out to be a man of character and honour. But his face will betray his shamefulness and his cowardice and he will say a word too many, constantly repeating what he has said. Now though his suit and shoes were worn, the guest who just left was brief of words and his eyes showed pride, and there was nothing shameful in his mien. For sure he is a man who has found some inner satisfaction far surpassing that of mere worldly goods. What he wishes to try out will be of no petty matter and I too have something to test on him. Also, if I were to give him the gold anyway, what is the point of asking his name?' said Byun, whereupon his children remained silent.

After obtaining the gold from Byun, Huh-Saeng did not return home but thought to himself:

'The town of Ansung lies at the point of conjunction of the provinces of Chungchung and Kyunggi and is the doorway to the three southern provinces. I will settle there.'

So deciding, he settled there and began buying up the entire stocks of jujubes, persimmons, chestnuts, pears, potatoes, pomegranates, oranges, lemons and other fruits and vegetables from the market at double the normal prices and stored them. Soon after Huh-Saeng had thus monopolized the fruit and vegetable market, no one in the country could hold feasts or offer ancestral rites for lack of necessary fruits. So a little later Huh-Saeng was able to sell his stocks to the same merchants who had first sold them to him at ten times the prices that he had paid. He then exclaimed:

'Hah! Since it is possible to undermine the entire economy of the nation with mere ten thousand gold pieces, it is not difficult to fathom the strengths and weaknesses of this nation.'

He then bought up in the same way all the knives, hoes, cotton, silk, wool and horsehair from Cheju Island — in other words all the materials needed for making men's hats and headbands.

'In a few years, no one in the country will be able to dress their hair for lack of headbands,' he said.

As he predicted, not many years passed before the price of headbands rose tenfold.

Huh-Saeng then said to an old boatman he happened to meet,

'Have you by any chance seen a desert island in the sea?'

'That I have, sir,' the boatman replied. 'Long time ago, I had been swept away by wind for three or four days to a desert island. I think it lay somewhere between the isles of Samun and Changgi. On the island, flowers bloomed and leaves grew luxuriant and all kinds of fruits and vegetables flourished by themselves, while herds of deer played and fish were not afraid of men.'

Huh-Saeng was overjoyed.

'If you take me to this place, you will share with me wealth and happiness,' he said to the boatman.

The boatman, taking Huh-Saeng's word for it, soon set sail and they sped south-eastward until they reached the island. Climbing to a high spot, Huh-Saeng surveyed the land below and said in a disappointed voice,

'The island measures not even a hundred leagues wide. The soil, however, seems rich and the water sweet, so I think I can at least play at being a rich old man here.'

But the boatman said to him,

'The island is uninhabited and there is no one within sight. From whom will you buy this land?'

'Where there is wisdom, there will also be men,' replied Huh. 'It is the lack of my wisdom and not of inhabitants that worries me.'

At about this time in a town called Byunsan, the people were being harassed by a band of robbers said to be some thousand strong. The provincial and county authorities had set soldiers after them but without success. The robbers themselves, however, were suffering from want as they could not freely go about to steal and plunder. Huh-Saeng leapt into the den of robbers and started reasoning with them.

'If you all together steal a thousand gold pieces, how many do you each get?' he asked them.

'We get only one gold piece each,' they answered.

'Have you wives?' Huh asked again.

'No.'

'Then have you any land?'

The robbers laughed at this.

'If we had wives and land, would we have taken the trouble to become thieves?'

'If what you say is true,' Huh said to them, 'then by getting yourselves wives and oxen and land, you can shed the dishonorable name of thief. You will also then be able to enjoy conjugal happiness and freely go abroad without fear of being arrested and so live happily ever after.'

'That is our wish too but we have no money,' they said. Huh-Saeng laughed at this and said to them,

'You seem to be as badly off as ever even after all your thieving. I will supply you with all the money you need. Go down to the sea tomorrow and you will see a ship flying a red flag. It will be full of gold. Take what you will from it.'

Thus promising the robbers, Huh-Saeng left them. The robbers, thinking him to be a madman, merely laughed at him.

Yet the next day they went down to the sea just out of curiosity. Waiting for them was Huh-Saeng and by him was a ship laden with three hundred thousand gold pieces. Amazed, they knelt and bowed as one man to Huh and said to him,

'From now on, we will follow your orders only, reverent sir.'

'Take as much as you want,' Huh said to them.

Upon this, the robbers crowded together to gather as much as they could but found that they could barely carry a hundred pieces each.

'Fine thieves you make when you can't even manage to carry off a hundred gold pieces each!' Huh said. 'Yet even if you were to wish for respectability, there is nowhere for you to go as your names are on the wanted list. So take one hundred pieces each, all of you, and bring back each a wife and an ox. I will wait for your return here.'

The thieves obeyed and dispersed.

Meanwhile, Huh-Saeng himself busied himself with procuring enough stock of grain to feed two thousand people for a whole year. On the appointed day, all the robbers returned, not one of them failing to turn up. They all got on boats with all their belongings and sailed to the island. The country was thus rid of these bandits and enjoyed peace and tranquility thereafter.

On the island, the robbers cut down the trees and built houses and with bamboo sticks raised hedges. As the soil was rich and fertile, everything thrived and flourished without needing any ploughing or weeding. Setting aside enough grain for three years, they took what remained to the island of Changgi — a small island belonging to Japan inhabited by some three hundred and ten thousand households. It so happened that in that particular year the harvest in the island was unprecedentedly poor; the robbers therefore had no difficulty getting rid of all their grain in return for which they received one million pieces in silver.

Huh-Saeng now exclaimed to himself,

'Now I have successfully tested a few things!'

He then summoned all the robbers and their wives, and said to them:

'When I first came to this island with you, I had wanted to create wealth first, then introduce learning and courtesy. But the land is small and I lack wisdom. So I will now leave this place. When your children grow old enough to hold a spoon, teach them to hold it in their right hands, and let the older, though he be older by one day only, eat before the younger.'

He then burnt all the boats saying, 'If no one goes, surely no one will come.'

He then threw five hundred thousand gold pieces into the sea saying, 'The day when the sea shall dry up, someone will be bound to find it. Since the entire nation cannot accommodate one million gold pieces, how can this small island cope with so much gold?'

Then intending to blot out all evil from the land, Huh-Saeng chose a man of some education as his companion and went around the whole island distributing gold to those in need.

After this, he found that he still had a hundred thousand pieces of gold left.

'With this, I will repay the debt I owe Byun,' Huh said.

Directly, Huh-Saeng went to seek Byun and asked him,

'Do you remember me?'

In great consternation, Byun said to him,

'You don't look as well as you did. Have you lost all the money I lent you?'

Huh-Saeng chuckled.

'Perhaps *you* allow wealth to affect your well-being? However precious gold is, how can it render a man more virtuous?' said he, handing Byun a bag containing the gold.

'My only regret is that the gold you lent me has become my shame as it has prevented me from completing my studies,' Huh-Saeng added.

Byun was greatly astonished at all this. He leapt up from his seat and bowing deeply before Huh refused the money except for the interest. Huh-Saeng was indignant.

'How dare you treat me like a tradesman?' he said and holding himself up proudly, he slammed out of the room.

Disarmed, the only thing that Byun could do was to secretly follow Huh. Huh-Saeng made for Namsan Hill and disappeared into a humble little hut. By the well nearby was an old woman doing her washing.

'Who lives in that hut?' Byun asked the old woman.

'It belongs to Huh-Saeng,' she replied. 'He was poor but loved learning beyond anything. It is five years since he left the house. Now his wife lives there alone and offers sacrifice on the day he left the house every year.'

Only then did Byun learn the name of this eccentric person to be Huh and he returned to his house in great admiration.

The following day, Byun took all the silver in the house and offered it to Huh-Saeng.

'If I had desired wealth, would I have cast away a hundred thousand gold pieces to obtain ten thousand?' Huh asked him. 'But from today I will rely on you for my daily bread and clothes; keep strictly to bare necessities, neither more nor less, and I will be content for the rest of my life. Why should a man trouble himself with worldly goods?' said Huh, refusing the silver.

Byun tried his best to dissuade Huh but there was no moving him. So from that day, Byun took it upon himself to personally bring whatever food and clothes he thought necessary and Huh too accepted these with glad countenance. But at a hint of anything extravagant exceeding his bare needs, Huh-Saeng would say in a disapproving voice,

'You will undo me in the end.'

When Byun appeared with a bottle of wine, however, Huh-Saeng would indeed be glad to see him and they would sit and drink to one another until they were both fairly merry. In this way several years went by and the friendship between them grew daily stronger.

One day Byun quietly asked Huh,

'How did you manage to make a hundred thousand gold pieces in five years?'

'It is not a difficult thing to guess. As you know, our country has no trade with other nations and even within the country, trade is none too brisk. So everything that is produced in the country is consumed in the country. A thousand pieces of gold is too small a sum of money to buy everything in the land but, divided into ten lots, you could purchase at least ten different kinds of merchandise. Dealing with ten items, even if you were to lose on one, you could make profit on nine others; it is the usual way of making profit and is the method used by small traders.

'But with ten thousand gold pieces, you can buy almost everything – the entire content of a cart, or of a ship, or even of a village. It is like casting hooked nets into the sea to sweep in all the fish. If you can thus quietly monopolize one product from the land or one kind of fish from the sea or one ingredient needed for medicine, you will paralyse all the merchants and cause them much annoyance. It is in truth a way of plaguing the people and if there should be anyone in later generations who uses this method, he will be doing the country an ill turn indeed.'

'How did you know in the first place that I would lend you the gold?'

'You would not have been the only one who would have given me the gold. I could have easily earned it myself but as our fate is in the hand of Heaven, how could I foresee that? He who uses me well is one favoured by Fortune and will surely enjoy greater wealth. Heaven has ordained this and, being so, how could he not give me the money? After I had obtained the gold, it was his luck which moved to make me successful. There is no knowing the outcome of the venture had I acted for myself only.'

Byun then said to him:

'At the moment, all the high government officials are vying with one another to restore the national honour fallen to disgrace. Now surely is the time for all wise scholars to come forth and show their wisdom. Then how is it that a man of your ability is content to remain in obscurity for the rest of your days?'

'How many men through the ages have lived and died in obscurity! Was not Cho Sung-gi able enough a man to be sent as ambassador to an enemy land and yet did he not live and die a commoner? Was not Yu Hyung-won too a man capable enough to command the army from one end of the country to another; yet did he not spend his life idly walking back and forth in some obscure little village? By that you can see what kind of men are running the country these days. As a successful merchant, I had earned enough wealth to buy nine kingdoms but had I not cast it all into the deep sea knowing only too well the vanity of all worldly things?'

At this, Byun took a deep breath and left the room.

Now Byun was on friendly terms with a high official called General Lee Whan, who was at that time the Commander-in-Chief of the Army.

One day talking with Byun, General Lee asked him,

'Is there a man of outstanding ability to be found anywhere in town?'

Byun promptly told him of Huh-Saeng. General Lee was greatly astonished and exclaimed,

'What an admirable person he sounds! What is his name?'

'I have known him for three years now but have never found out his full name,' replied Byun.

'He must indeed be a genius. Let's go and seek him out at once.'

Refusing all attendance, General Lee and Byun set out on foot to Huh-Saeng's house. Upon arriving, Byun persuaded General Lee to wait outside while he went in first to acquaint Huh of General Lee's coming.

Huh-Saeng, however, hardly listened at all, showing interest only in the bottle of wine that Byun brought.

'Come, let's quickly uncork the bottle,' he said.

Then making himself comfortable, he drank merrily with Byun. Byun felt very sorry for General Lee thus kept waiting outside for so long and reminded Huh several times of his presence but to no avail. The night deepened. At last Huh-Saeng said,

'Well, let's see the guest.'

General Lee came in but Huh did not even bother to rise from his seat. Acutely uncomfortable, General Lee did not know where to put himself and hurriedly told Huh the reason for his coming. Waving his hand, Huh then said to him,

'The night is short and your words are long and tedious. What is your position at the moment?'

'I am a general,' replied General Lee.

'Then you must be a trusted subject of His Majesty. If I were to recommend you a person of great wisdom, would you be able to persuade His Majesty to come personally to him to beg him to take office?'

General Lee sat with his head bent; after a while he said,

'That would not be an easy matter. What is your next request?'

'I have yet to be content with the second best,' Huh replied, 'but since you insist, I will tell you. As you know, many soldiers of the Ming Dynasty of China had in the old days received much favour from this land and as a result, many of their offspring have moved east to settle here. These men are now wandering round the land suffering hardship as they cannot find anyone to wed them. Would it be in your power to render them a great service by asking His Majesty to send out the daughters of the Royal Family and of high officials to take these men as their husbands?'

Again General Lee was silent; at last he uttered,

'That would not be possible.'

'It appears to me that there is very little that you can do,' Huh-Saeng said. 'There is one last thing which I don't think would be too difficult a matter to arrange. I wonder whether you would be able to carry out that last one?' So saying he continued:

'It is said that if one were to stand up for a noble cause, one has first to establish friendship with great men. In the same way, were one to invade another country, it is not possible to do so without using spies. Has not Manchuria of a sudden become so mighty an empire as to boast that it has not yet had time to make friends with the Chinese people? In this situation, if our country should take the initiative to surrender first, would they not look kindly upon us and trust us? Then we could ask them to allow our children to further their studies in their land and following the old tradition of the Tang and Yuan Dynasties even let them sit for their Civil Service Examination. Also we could ask them to let our merchants pass freely into their country and they are sure to be pleased with our overtures of friendship and welcome our suggestions.

'We could then select some of our young people and after dressing them up in Chinese clothes and cutting their hair, let the educated ones sit for the Chinese Civil Service Examination while those of low birth could pass into the southern province as merchants. Mingling freely with the Chinese, they would then spy out all the strong and weak points of the enemy and make alliance with great men there. Only then can we plan our great scheme to conquer their land and save the tarnished honour of the country.

'We would then select an emperor for the kingdom. If we cannot find a man with the name of Chou, a descendent of the Royal Family of the Ming Dynasty, then we would summon all the lords and Heaven will elect the ordained one. If all goes well, our country will be able to play mentor to a great nation. If not, we would still have the pleasure of being the most powerful lord.'

Hearing this, General Lee said in a dejected voice,

'The high officials these days are so busy observing proprieties that none will dare cut their hair and don Chinese clothes.'

Huh-Saeng raised his voice at this:

'Who are these so-called "high officials"? How dare they take the liberty of calling themselves "high officials" when they are in truth nothing but barbarians? The white suit that they wear is nothing but mourning clothes and the way they tie up their hair in a knot on top of their heads is a barbarian custom. The hero Byun Ok-gi of old days had no scruple in shaving his head in order to redress his personal grievance, nor did King Muryung of Cho Kingdom feel any shame in donning barbarian garments in order to build a stronger nation. But you who call yourselves "high officials", while claiming to avenge the national disgrace in obedience to the Royal Command, are afraid to hurt even a hair on your precious heads. Nor are you willing to alter those wide sleeves of yours which make it impossible for you to engage in military training. When you should be busy devoting yourselves to various martial arts, such as horse riding, spear-throwing and archery, all you do is cling on to your impractical wide sleeves. Behaving in this unseemly manner, how dare you say this and that about proper behaviour?

'For the first time in my life, I have told you the ways of practising ruse, but you who call yourself a trusted subject can carry out not one of them. Such a fellow richly deserves to die,' Huh said, looking round for a sword.

General Lee, leaping to his feet in great fear, bolted through the back window and ran all the way home as fast as his legs could carry him.

The next day he went to call on Huh-Saeng again but Huh-Saeng had already vanished.

translated by Moon Hi Kyung

The Tale of a *Yangban*[1]

There lived in a village called *Jungsun* a yangban. He was virtuous and deeply loved learning. Everytime a new magistrate came to take office in the village, the yangban personally called on him to pay his respects. But he was very poor and for several years lived on what the government lent out, at the end of which he found himself in debt by about a thousand sacks of rice.

One day the Governor of the Province visited the village on an inspection tour. While going over the accounts of the local office, he found the debt left unpaid by the yangban and was extremely indignant.

'Who is this yangban who has thus eaten up so much of the military provision?' he said, immediately ordering the yangban to be put under arrest.

The magistrate was a kind-hearted man.

'How pitiful his position is. And where would he find the money to pay the debt?' he said, reluctant to throw the yangban into prison, but there was no way he could avoid it.

Tha yangban, meanwhile, merely wept a little without being able to find a way out of the dreadful situation he was in. Seeing such a pitiful state of affairs, the wife of the yangban felt only exasperation.

'It seems to me that you have wasted your life reading useless books. Since you can't even raise such a paltry sum of money, your being a yangban is not worth a groat,' she said clicking her tongue.

At that time in the same village lived an immensely rich man who, though accredited to be richer than anyone, had no social distinction. When the man heard the story, he hurriedly

[1] *Yangban* is a title of distinction given to a man of upper class, in other words a gentleman.

called his family together for consultation.

'However poor a man is, with the title of yangban he is always honoured and respected. We are richer than anyone here but daily we fall lower in the eyes of the world. Never once can we ride through the streets holding up our heads proudly and if we see a yangban coming, we have to suffer the indignity of having to grovel and crawl on our knees to prostrate ourselves on the ground before him. I have heard that a certain yangban is having much difficulty paying his debt. Since he will not be able to maintain his position as a yangban in his present circumstances, I will offer to buy his position from him,' he said.

The man immediately sought the yangban's house and, telling him of what he had in mind, offered to pay his debt for him. The yangban was overjoyed and agreed without a moment's hesitation, whereupon the man immediately remitted to the local office a thousand sacks of rice.

When the magistrate saw this, he was much taken by surprise and started for the yangban's house to congratulate him on this happy turn of affairs and to ask him how he had managed to repay the debt. But to his great astonishment, he found the yangban prostrate on the ground calling him, 'Sir, sir,' in a pair of coarsely woven half-trousers and a shapeless hat such as the ones worn by men of mean birth. The magistrate leapt down to the yard and, taking him by the sleeve asked him,

'Sir, why do you lower yourself so?'

Even more overwhelmed by this, the yangban did not know where to put himself and prostrated himself even more.

'You do me a great honour, sir. May I humbly inform you that I am not acting like this without a good reason? I have sold the position of yangban to the richman of the village, sir. That being the case, how could I be brazen-faced enough to play yangban again?'

Upon hearing this, the magistrate exclaimed in admiration.

'Ah! The richman has done a noble deed, indeed. It was a truly gentlemanly action. To have wealth and yet not to be enslaved by it is to love justice; to courageously help those in need is virtue; and to hate what is low and love what is high surely is wisdom. He must be a true yangban.

'But to let a matter of such importance be carried out only

between the two without any deed of the transaction may be a source of legal dispute later on. I will summon all the people of the village as witnesses and draw out a deed upon which I will set my personal seal.'

He then returned to his office and called all the gentry, peasants, artisans and tradesmen. Seating the richman at the right hand of the chief official and placing the yangban next to the secretary, he started to draw out the deed:

'In September of the twenty-first year of King Yongjo's reign, I hereby proclaim as follows:

'It happened that the title of yangban has been sold to pay the debt, the amount of which comes exactly to a thousand sacks of rice. There are several different names for yangban. He who buries himself in studies is called *suhn-bi*; he who serves in the government *daebu*; and he who possesses outstanding wisdom *kunja*. Now the root sense of the word "yangban" means "both ranks", referring both to the military rank which lies to the west and the civil rank which lies to the east. These two together are called "yangban".

'For the richman here, I will choose whatever name of yangban I deem fit. But from today, he shall cease all lowly conduct, and imitating the decorum of the men of old, behave as it befits a yangban. Everyday, he shall rise before dawn and light the lamp; after which he shall sit staring down at his nose for a while and collect his thoughts together. Then sitting on his knees with both heels together, he should be able to recite without any difficulty passages from old Chinese classics; and he shall never utter the word poverty however cold and hungry he is. He shall also beat his upper set of teeth against the lower and blow his nose by flicking the back of his head with his fingers. Everytime he feels like spitting, he shall slowly swallow it and when putting on a fur hat, he shall brush it with his sleeves to make it clean and fluffy.

'When he washes his face, he will not rub his face with his fist nor shall he brush his teeth too violently. When he calls his slaves, either male or female, he shall call in a low dignified voice and when he walks, he shall take slow stately steps brushing his heels against the ground. He should also be able to copy in writing old classics and Chinese poems from the Chung Era, fitting a hundred words in a line. Never shall he hold any money in his hands, nor ask about the price of rice, nor take off his clothes however hot it is. He shall not sit at table hatless nor shall he, during dinner, gulp down the soup. Were he to drink soup, he shall not slurp nor shall he bang his chopsticks when he puts them down on the table. Moreover, he will not eat raw onions to make his breath smell, nor suck his beard after drinking rice wine, nor suck his pipe so hard as to make his cheeks sink in.

'However angry he is, he will never beat his wife nor throw dishes at her. He will also not beat children with his bare hands, nor beat the slaves to death however much wrong they have done him. Though he should scold the cow, he shall not find fault with the man who sold him the cow; he shall call in neither the shamans when he is ill nor any monks when holding ancestral rites. However cold he is, he shall not warm his hands by the fire, spit in someone's face while conversing, become a butcher nor gamble indiscriminately.

'I hereby certify that should there be any violations to these rules above, the yangban will be permitted to file a law suit against the richman at the county court.

'On September of the twenty-first year of King Yongjo's reign I witness this deed, sealed by the official Seal of the Magistrate of Jungsun village, attested by county officials *Chasu* and *Byulgam*.'[2]

Then the errand-boy fetched the Seal and stamped the deed. The thumping of the heavy Seal on the deed mingled with the sound of the village drum announcing the hour and the sight of the Seal on the deed looked no different from the Great Bear sprawled out on the page or some stars stuck there at random.

The richman stood tongue-tied for a while and uttered at last, 'Is this all there is to it? I have heard that a yangban is no different from a heavenly being, but if this is all it is, then I have been grossly deceived into paying so much for it. I beg you to alter it a little to my advantage, sir.'

The magistrate, deciding to grant his wish, agreed to rewrite the deed.

'When Heaven created the nation, he separated the people into four classes. Of the four the most honourable class was

[2] *Chasu* and *Byulgam*: titles of minor officials at the provincial government office.

that of scholars or *suhn-bi* and this he called the yangban. There being none greater than a *suhn-bi* in this world, he does not have to till the land nor deal in trade but has merely to know something of old classical writings or history. He will then sit for the Civil Service Examination which, if he passes with distinction, will make him a high government official. Even if not, he can be assured at least of the post of *Jinsa*[3] in the province.

'What is more, though the certificate given to a *suhn-bi* who has distinguished himself at the Civil Service Examination measures not two lengths long and looks but trifling, it is in reality no different from a bag of gold as all kinds of wonderful things come out of it. As for a *suhn-bi* who has been made a *Jinsa*, though he distinguish himself at the age of thirty, it will not be too late for him to make a name for himself. If he happens to have the good fortune to find favour in the eyes of anyone who is in power, then as a bailiff he will enjoy all sorts of luxury and soon acquire a pot belly. Also deep in his room, he will be able to while away his time with courtesans, and grain-sacks piled high in his yard will be food for his pet cranes.

'Even an impecunious *suhn-bi* living in the country can behave in a despotic manner. Though he should borrow the next-door neighbour's ox to plough his land first and get the village peasants to weed his fields, who will dare find fault with him? Even if he pours lye down your nose, mess up your hair, and pluck your beard from your chin, you will have no one to complain to.'

The deed was almost half completed. The richman, flabbergasted, stammered,

'Ah, stop, sir! I beg you, stop! It is preposterous. Why don't you tell me to become a thief rather.' Then shaking his head, he went away as fast as he could.

After this, the richman never uttered the word yangban agains for the rest of his life.

translated by Moon Hi-Kyung

[3] Jinsa: a title given to a yangban who has passed the first stage of the Civil Service Examination.

Samsolgi

Samsolgi is a collection of nine allegorical stories in three volumes, though six are known and identified, it is generally believed to have been published in the late nineteenth century. The name of the author is not known and there is some debate over the number of stories the volumes contain. 'The Stork Decides the Case' is the seventh story, which comes from an original manuscript in the British Museum. Its existence has not been widely known.

The Stork Decides a Case

Long ago, somewhere in Kyŏngsang province there lived a man who had inherited wealth. His harvest every year was more than ten thousand bagfuls, so it may readily be realised how boundless were his blessings. He was comfortably provided with a fortune for life, and there was nothing more he desired. Besides this, there was not one of his neighbours who would not praise his goodness.

However, one of his own family was a depraved, unprincipled fellow, a stupid drifter. One day he arrived unexpectedly and ranted at him: 'You are living very well. Your good life is entirely your inheritance and we are both from the same great-great-grandfather, so should I not feel galled that you are the only one who has plenty to eat and wear and lacks nothing? If you now divide that property between us, nothing will happen to you, but if you do not, I will make your life impossible.'

He ranted on all night without stopping, and even went so far as to try starting a fire. When the people of the neighbourhood saw his conduct and reckoned up how wicked the fellow was, they were vexed beyond bearing. They privately urged the rich master not just to let him go on. 'Would it not be better,' they said, 'to petition the village head or appeal to the provincial governor to put a stop to such things?'

The rich man listened to them and thought they were right.

'It will not be an easy matter dealing with this fellow. I shall go up to the capital and petition the Board of Punishments to make sure that that is the end of the trouble,' he said, and took the fellow with him up to the capital.

Now this rich man, though he lived far away in the country, could read fairly well, and his wide reading at all times gave him a fair degree of fluency and a proud style too. Faced with his present situation, he was fully determined to win his suit. He was vexed and mortified beyond bearing, and determined to have this fellow brought to justice, so that he would not be able to make any further move. He came up to Seoul, found the Board of Punishments, and presented his deposition:

'I live in such-and-such a township in Kŏngsang Province, and by good fortune have abundant worldly goods. Naturally I help many poor people among my relations, but there is one fellow of my own family who, by his frivolity and dissoluteness, squandered his family's wealth and drifted all over the place. I took pity on him because of this. I built him a house again, bought him land, and tried every way I could manage to give him a living, but he grows more and more monstrous. He did not work his land, but just enjoyed every idle pursuit and drinking. He did not conserve his possessions for his family, but sold them all in a morning, until he had nothing left. Then he delighted in wandering around without any fixed abode, so now, if I give him some capital to set up, for instance, as a merchant, somehow he gets through it all. Sometimes he comes back from his wanderings within a year and takes goods, and sometimes he comes within two years and makes me pay out two or three hundred pieces of gold, or four or five hundred pieces of gold. It has happened countless times, but lately it has been worse. He has become a real villain. He visited me and raved at me time and time again, and abused me terribly. He said that, if I did not divide up my property and land equally between us, he would kill me and do away with me. He quarrels every day, and tried to set fire to my house. You could not find another such fellow anywhere in the world. I cannot bear it, and have come all this way to present a detailed petition to this just court. Your honour, I abase myself before you and pray: it is my earnest hope that you will in future take special measures against this uprincipled fellow, and make life bearable for a citizen of a far off country district.'

The magistrate read the petition carefully, and ordered the clerk to say that judgment would be given at a session on a later day. The criminal had not yet been examined, but the rich man just waited for the session to take place in a few days. In the meantime he could have visited the clerks and got a hint perhaps, but he was completely convinced himself that he had done nothing wrong. He visited no one at all. He felt unbearably mortified, and just looked forward to the fellow's being dealt with.

Now the fellow may have enjoyed his idle pursuits, and may have been frivolous and unprincipled, but, in getting around the world, he had gained wide experience, and, besides, he was aware of the way things were in this day and age. He had come up for the law suit, but at the same time had visited his cronies too. He had found his way to favour at the Board of Punishments, and got on his side the officials, high and low, and even the clerks and messengers. It has always been the case in law suits that, if one is quick to see the signs, one can win even an impossible case without any trouble at all. This is what is meant by 'writing the square character *wal*, "to say", on a deerskin': it can be changed to the oblong characer *il*, 'sun', that is the meaning can be changed by stretching the skin.

Anyway, when the day of the session arrived, the higher officials sat round in a circle, the lower officials sat in a long line across, and the clerks took their places sitting on the edges of the earth verandah. It was incomparably impressive. The order was given to the messengers to call in both parties, and they were made to kneel at the foot of the steps. This was the order made:

'Now hear this. Rich man, nowhere in the world can there be such a cruel fellow as you. Even a man who has made his own fortune feeds the poor and helps the wretched. Much more should you, who have become a millionaire with your family business and your riches acquired through the generations, easily afford even to distribute rice to the people of your whole township in a year of famine. But you do not help your relations. You bring cases against them to try to drive them away. Nowhere in the world is there such an unprincipled fellow as you. Do you not feel any guilt in your heart that one cousin is eating well and another cousin is starving close to death? If we took account of your deeds, it would be appropriate to bring you to justice, but you are completely forgiven. The case is simply dismissed and rejected, and that is a greater kindness than you deserve. You are to make the division as he asked you to, and let there be no quarrelling between relatives.

'A written promise to this effect is to be got from him before he is released.'

When the rich man thought about it, he was mortified and vexed beyond bearing that he had lost his case. By asking favours, that unprincipled fellow was actually going home justified as a good man, while a generous person like himself was being dismissed as an undischarged criminal. He felt as if his heart would burst, and he wondered whether it would be likely to have any effect if he stated the whole case again. He knelt up again and tried to make a statement, but there was an icy roar of disapproval and they tried to push him in the back and remove him.

'If I try to speak out in court,' the rich man thought, 'and tell them the whole affair from the beginning to end, they will certainly say that it is contempt of court. They will probably arrest me without compunction, and treat me according to the law. If those stupid messengers are determined to beat me, I shall not be able to go home, and shall only be bruised for life. What should I do?'

He thought this, that and every way, but his heart was full of vexation and sadness at the thought that he must go home having lost his case. He looked up at the magistrate, scrutinizing him carefully, and then he had a sudden thought. He certainly had to go home having lost his case, but if he made up a story and told it quietly, and if those fellows only listened, they would be bound to lose face at least. So he stood up again, sat down near the foot of the steps and said:

'I have come all this way to the capital, and have lost my case. I am going home, but I have a story which is worth your hearing, so I desire that you hear it.'

When the officials heard this, they thought it most ridiculous, but, since they always liked to hear a story, they wondered whether a country story might be amusing, so they wanted to hear it. However, if they listened to this fellow's story instead of settling the other cases, others might regard it as a loss of dignity for them, so they pretended to scold him as they gave their order:

'You live in the country and do not understand the importance of proper respect. It is improper of you to suggest telling a story in court, but we shall at least grant your request. Tell us what you have to say.'

After they had finished, the rich man cleared his throat and spoke:

'Once upon a time, an oriole, a cuckoo and an ibis were siting down together arguing whose singing was the best. They went on for several days without coming to a decision, and then one day the oriole said, "Let us not quarrel between ourselves. Let us take it to court."

'"As I have heard," one of the creatures replied, "the stork is the tallest of all the feathered creatures, his beak the longest, and his body the most august. He has keen powers of judgment and does everything most correctly. Because of this they call him 'General Stork', so why do we not visit that General Stork and get him to give a decision on our voices?"

'They all thought this best, and agreed formally to do so, but the one of them called the ibis, who had a terrible voice, though he was very clever, went home and thought, "I spoke confidently, but of the three voices, mine is the most disagreeable, I think. If anyone asked me, I would say that I was the most certain to lose. There is an old saying, 'Man may make plans, Heaven grants success,' so anyway, if I do some soliciting, it must do me some good."

'So a plan formed in his mind. All night he went round the river banks and the paddy field dikes, and the pools and creeks, wandering all over the place, collecting things which the stork had enjoyed all his life. He collected food of every sort — roes, frogs, water snails, toads, tadpoles, leeches, snakes, cicada grubs, worms, maggots, earwigs, house-fly grubs, and so on. He arranged them attractively and tidily in a well shaped red gourd, and took them to the stork's house.

'When he got there, he rushed in through the main gate, stepped in through the inner gate, crept up the steps, and laid them down humbly on the verandah of the grand pavilion. He called the steward in a peremptory tone to take his compliments to the master.

'Now it was just the time of the first full moon of the summer. By day the stork was immersed in public affairs, and could not properly take a nap, and, when night came, he was pestered by people who came to him for help until midnight and into the early hours. He had only just got to sleep when the sound of someone calling the steward woke him up with a shock. He listened quietly, and realised that it was the ibis.

‘“I cannot think why that fellow has come to my house. He has always treated me very casually before, and now, in the middle of the night, here he is, suddenly arrived right at my private room. He has brought me some gifts, and is telling my man to present his compliments. It must be because I have got some position lately that he has barged his way in here. He is up to something. He must have come up against some difficulty, and got himself in a fix, and that is why he has come to ask me a favour, I should think. But I had better see what there is in it for me first.”

‘He pretended to groan, sat up, put a red half-quilt round his shoulders, and looked carefully in the light of the lamp. There he saw all sorts of things, all of them essentials — things fit to be dried, stored away and used in religious ceremonies, things to send in lunch boxes when the young gentlemen went out into the arena to take their examinations as tips, things to be given on a Japanese platter as tokens of respect to new in-laws, things to be kept at home to soothe the babies when they cried, things to whet the appetite of anyone who was badly sick, and even things for feasting guests at birthday parties. They were all things that the stork could make good use of. He was so thrilled and pleased with them that he told the steward to put them away safely before he gave a long drawn out cry.

‘“It is a long time since I heard your voice. How inconsiderate you are. How have you been? And how have your mother and everybody been? I am really glad to see you. I did not know what had become of you, and was worried no end. Seeing you here tonight is like meeting someone who has been dead. But you cut yourself off from us and stopped coming here without a word of explanation — what was the meaning of it? That is a most unreliable way to carry on. Now here you are in the middle of the night. What is the emergency? Tell me, and, whatever it is, you will have my sympathy. I shall see that nothing happens to you, and shall make you happy again.”

‘Now the ibis had known that it had been several years since he had paid his respects, and that he was also being a nuisance waking someone up from a sound sleep in the middle of the night. He had feared that if the stork got angry with him he might have been pecked terribly by that long beak. But he had not. Only when he saw that he was calling him in a very friendly way and talking to him as if he were glad to see him did he come right up to the door.

'"I have had my trifling troubles lately," he said, "and I have been busy too night and day with the business of making a living. That is why I have not been able to pay my respects for a long time. Now I have come to pay my respects, and I am so overwhelmed that I do not know what to say, except that there is an emergency, and that is why I have come like this, guilty as I feel. I am more sorry than I can say for my impertinence."

'The stork gave a languid laugh. "I knew you had come to see me because you had some such emergency — why else should you have come? But tell me exactly what it is and what is on your mind."

'"Well, I'll come to the point," the ibis told him. "The oriole, the cuckoo and I had a singing contest between the three of us, but, as they say, 'no one realises his own mistakes,' and we could not decide the places in the contest. Not being able to come to any conclusion, we discussed it among ourselves, and decided that since you, General, were extremely discerning in your judgment, we should gather at your house tomorrow and have a trial. Now, since my voice is the most terrible of the three of ours, I was in a quandary. I was certain not to win in the trial, so I thought, in my own stupid way, that perhaps by telling your honour the circumstances first, and putting my request to you, I might try to beat the other two. I hope that your honour may not have forgotten our former friendship, and that in the trial tomorrow you might be good enough to turn my mark in Chinese upside down so that it reads 'top' instead of 'bottom'."

'When the stork heard this, he felt very reassured.

'"The lower classes are always stupid like this, and know nothing of proper respect. You think only of what you want yourselves. You imagine that anything is easy. In law suit, generally speaking, if one allows one's personal feelings to enter into it, complaints are made, and frequent unreasonable litigation injures the body politic. You would not understand such things, but if winning is not a matter of working out rights and wrongs, but a conspiracy to deceive, that is what is called 'a bell that can be hung either on the ear or the nose' — a thing that serves any purpose you put it to. How could I deal with your affair with so little conscience? You have had a lot of favours from me in the past, but in this case, however hard I work for you, if I give the victory to your voice, they are bound to say that I was influenced to misconduct a public affair, and then I might be discredited completely. That is what worries me."

'The ibis changed his tune. "If that is your command, I take my leave of you, thanking you for your great kindness."

'The stork laughed as he said, "How can one know anything in this world before it is accomplished? Let us just see." The ibis took his leave and went home.

'At dawn the three creatures gathered at the stork's house, and the case began. The stork took his seat on the verandah, and a countless host of birds took up their places to right and left. The eagle was the Clerk of Laws, the kite, the crow, the magpie, the osprey, the hawk and the goose were the Six Departmental Clerks, and the heron, the tawny owl, the nightjar, the pigeon, the long-eared owl, the swallow, the sparrow and the rest were marshalled to right and left. The three fellows were called in. They came in at the same time, swooped their wings and said,

'"We had a voice contest, and were unable to judge the places, so, with the axe hanging over our heads, we present our case before your honour, trusting in your discernment in giving judgments."

'The stork, with a solmen face, ordered:

'"If that is what you wish to do, each of you sing. After you have let me hear you, I shall decide who is top and who is bottom."

'The oriole flew in first, and sang this beautiful song:

'"This is my song:

'"In the good season when spring is at its best
'"The plum and peach blossom are in full bloom,
'"The green of the willows on the front stream
'"Hangs like a herb-green curtain,
'"The green of the willows on the back stream
'"Hangs like a salex-green curtain.
'"This is when my body, coloured like gold,
'"Flies in and glides in,

'"Enjoying the sky at sunset,
'"And my delicate voice, crystal-clear,
'"Is blown away on the spring breeze.
'"Who, through the ninety days of spring,
'"Would not think me beautiful?"

'As soon as the stork heard this, he knew that it was, as the oriole had said, extremely beautiful, but if he now said that his voice was best, he would have to give back to the ibis the bribes he had received with his request. If he said that it was not nice, his lack of propriety would injure the body politic. After muttering to himself over it, he gave his decision:

'"Now hear this. A T'ang poet said, 'Chase away the little oriole. Teach it not to sing on the branch.' Your voice may be beautiful, but it is frail and ineffective."

'The oriole withdrew in some shame, and the cuckoo came in next. He tuned up his vocal cords, and sang in an exquisite voice:

'"This is my song:

'"Deep in the thousand mountains green with trees
'"The countless gorges and peaks are mysterious.
'"The mists rise and turn to clouds,
'"The clouds roll and all form peaks.
'"Another world is created.
'"Ten mile high waterfalls flow down
'"And hang like crystalled curtains.
'"The wind soughs in the pine trees,
'"The moon is bright on the autumn paulownias.
'"This delicate voice of mine.
'"Deep in the mountains, is both singer and accompanist.
'"Who would be glad to hear it?"

'The stork listened and then gave his next judgment:

'"It has been said, 'The cuckoo sings at moonset of the furthest separation in the world.' Your voice may be refreshingly clear, but it is completely poverty-stricken. When I think of our past friendship, I may well feel sorry."

'The cuckoo withdrew in his turn, unsuccessful, and then the ibis flew in to sing, but when he thought of how better voices than his had already lost and withdrawn, he did not know what to do. He was too ashamed to open his mouth, but, trusting that he had sweetened the stork, he lower his head and just muttered,

' "I have only one cry, I can only croak my name, 'Ttaok'. I have no other way of expressing myself, and so I trust to your honour's judgment."

'The stork was surprised to hear this, and slapped his knees in joy. "What a fine fellow, a splendid fellow! You have the dignity of General Hsiang of old, of whom it is said in the Historical Records that a thousand perished at one quick word of anger of his. You have the roar of anger of Chang T-te that drove back a million troops at the Chang-pan Bridge, as we read in the Romance of the Three Kingdoms. Your voice is the grandest, and your disposition that of a true hero."

'That was his decision, that the ibis' voice was the top voice. That was the sort of creature he was: he took his bribe and gave his stubborn false decision. He was unjust to the oriole and the cuckoo. Shall not his sins be visited upon his children and grand-children? Since such creatures behave so wrongly, because they are immersed in worldly desires, did you not regard such fellows as sons of dogs and children of oxen? You were amused at them, but now the judiciary in the capital too is just the same. My own case is finished, so I have spoken uselessly and to no effect, and now I withdraw.'

The officials of the Board of Punishments had no words to offer in reply, and were thoroughly ashamed.

translated by W.E. Skillend

Korean Poetic Tradition and the Sijo

CHUNG CHONG-WHA

The history of poetry in Korea goes back as far as 17 B.C. when King Yuri of the kingdom of Kokuryo wrote the Song of Yellow Birds:

Yellow birds play around,
Male and female together.
How painful that I'm alone.
Who do I return home with?

King Yuri, when he lost his first wife, remarried to two Chinese sisters, Hwahi and Chihi, who became jealous of each other and quarrelled often. In the end, the youngest one returned to China. The grieved king composed this poem when he saw a pair of courting warblers on a tree.

This poem is among the earliest written evidence of Korean poetic tradition. It is written in Chinese, and therefore it is also one of the very first works representing Korean poetry in Chinese. In fact, the early Korean poetic tradition was nurtured and developed in this mode. It was natural that poetic sentiment was expressed in Chinese. Until the invention of the Korean alphabet, Hangul, in 1446, Chinese was the official and only language that Koreans used not only to express the poetic mood and entertaining fictional stories, but also to run and manage the state, public and private affairs. Chinese was not only the official expression to preserve the government records but also to test the qualification of government officials. Civil servants at national examinations had to not only recite correctly the Chinese classics but to compose poetry in Chinese as well.

Of course there was the vernacular tradition of literature, and this goes back much, much earlier. In the time of Puyo (1 B.C.–A.D. 300), according to Chinese records, people observed a special festivity in January when they gathered together, drank, danced and sang for a few days in a row. This tells that there was music and poetry and it is most likely that poetry was in the vernacular tongue. If Chinese was a vehicle for more refined sentiments and for learned occasions, the vernacular tongue was a more natural means of giving vent to spontaneous expressions.

It is not quite clear when exactly the Chinese language came to Korea. The rough date is presumed to be around the 1st century, although there is no way of verifying this theory. Certainly around the 5th and the 6th centuries the language was in use. Some Chinese records reveal that in the 30th year of King Kungocho (A.D. 375) of Paekje (18 B.C.–A.D. 660) government records in Chinese characters were preserved in the royal archive, and in the 6th year of King Chinbeung (546) of Shilla the national history was compiled in Chinese. The famous Manchurian monument of King Kwang-gaeto of Kokury with the controversial inscriptions in Chinese was erected in 441.

Yidu testifies the Korean reliance on Chinese. It was invented in the 6th century and was widely in circulation in the kingdom of Shilla. It was a scholaristic attempt to adapt the foreign language for local use, mixing Chinese mostly with Korean particles. It made the reading of Chinese texts easy. It also made the writing easy. It was a kind of pidgin English of the time. In *Yidu* a large volume of poetry was written, which was called *Hyangga*, the home song, as against the poetry of China. It was a kind of pop song of the time. Hyangga was in a strict sense different from Yidu, in that it transcribed Korean expressions by using Chinese characters and sounds. Luckily some songs of Hyangga still survive, like the famous Song of Cho-yong:

Under the bright moonlight in the capital city
I caroused late at night.
When I returned to my chamber
Lo, there are four legs in my bed!

Two are mine;
Whose legs are the other two?
Even though the two were once mine
What can I do when they are taken away?

Cho-yong is a mythical figure, attributed to be a son of the Dragon King, but most likely to be in a realistic term a foreigner who looked different from the native people. The song is about the man being cuckolded, but unlike the typical Korean male he takes the situation poetically and resigns to it, without making a jealous scene. This magnanimous gesture inspired poets, and it was later developed into a folk dance. The poem itself has folkloric elements, which distinguishes itself from the lofty sentiments channelled into poems written in Chinese by the Confucian scholar cum civil servants whose ethical code was never allowed moral diversions.

However, in spite of local attempts to accommodate the popular sentiments in poetry, the Korean poetic tradition developed for a long time along the line of Chinese poetry. Practitioners of the art were largely scholars and civil servants, who expressed only 'proper' feelings in all forms of Chinese poetic tradition. Even long after the invention of Hangul, this practice persisted. The vernacular language was for the most part left for the expression of 'common' feeling and for women and the common people. In a sense, this attitude lasted until the end of the Yi Dynasty at the beginning of the 20th century. The Korean poetry in Chinese was more legitimate, whereas the poetry in the vernacular language was secondary. If the former represented a formal side of Korean culture, the latter represented an informal and therefore deeper layer of Korean mentality. Very often the poetry in Chinese did not have visible human faces, nor did it have strong human feelings directly reflected. The subjects of these poems were the love of nature, inspired by majestic natural sceneries or melancholic scenes of natural phenomena such as the setting sun on the pine tree or desolate autumn evenings. There are no daring imageries, nor powerful evocation of emotions. There is no bold confession of erotic feelings. Consequently the poetry in Chinese is rather stiff and less lively.

For more candid and direct human feelings one has to go to

the poems in the vernacular language. Here is a poem about a faithless lover.

I wish I could cut out the waist of this deep mid-winter night
And curl it softly, softly under the warm spring quilt;
And slowly, slowly spread it on the night my love comes
back.

This poem is written by a kiseang girl (close to a Japanese geisha) in the 16th century. Nothing is much known about Hwang Jinie, except that she was a legendary beauty in the city of Kaesung, the capital of the Koryo Dynasty, and that she belonged in her social status to the humble class of professional hostesses. She was also a very sensitive poet and left many poems behind along with many stories of her seduction of great scholars. The fact that Hwang compared a long winter night to a man's body is a bold challenge to the formal tradition of poetry. The girl waited, in vain, for her faithless lover to come and make love to her in that long, long mid-winter night. The man did not make it and she said to herself: 'Well, he did not come. I'll cut out the middle part of this night (she uses words like "waist" of the "night") and keep it in the light spring quilt for another night when he really comes to my bed.' The whole poem is constructed with rather daring sensual imageries, which are not to be found in the other formal tradition.

Hwang Jinie's love-poem is a work of fine craftsmanship; it is much more artistic and refined compared with the other love poems written in the vernacular language. Here is one whose author is unknown. It is an erotic poem almost to the degree of being vulgar.

Lady, heat for sale! Early summer heat for sale!
Late summer heat for sale!
The heat of many summers and winters for sale!

Mid-summer night heat that burnt my whole intestines
And made me pant and sweat on a moonlit bed
While legs and arms entangled; that is for sale!
The long mid-winter night heat that burnt my throat
And made me drink the cold rice water in one gulp

After two bodies had become one in a thick quilt in a warm room,
And had become almost out of breath; that is for sale, Lady!

Dear man, among your goods, who would refuse the two love heats?
Please, don't sell it to others. Let me buy them.

The fact that the author is anonymous and that the sentiment is rather coarse makes the poem a kind of folk literature. The form also indicates this. The original sijo is strictly composed in three lines with 45 syllables (or characters) altogether. Diversions to this rigid rule were allowed only in the 18th century when folk literature began to rise and when many erotic poems were written anonymously and recited (or sung) among the common people.

The origin of the sijo is not precisely known, and there has not been much research done on the subject. All that is known is that it was started around the 13th century at the end of the Koryo Dynasty, not by the common people, but by a group of Confucian scholars who had a fine sense of poetry possibly from their practice in their Chinese language poems. The common theme of the sijo at the time was rather Confucian in nature and close to that of the other, formal tradition. Won Chun-suk's poem testifies to this.

Who calls the bamboo bent that bends under the snow?
If it were bent, would it be green in the white?
You are the only one who keeps up in the coldest winter days.

Won, whose exact dates of birth and death are unfortunately not traceable, served the Koryo Dynasty and refused to work for the new dynasty of Yi Sung-gye. Choi Young (1316–1388), one of the great generals of the last phase of the Koryo Dynasty, also expressed the similar sentiment in the similar mode:

Do not laugh at the pine; it is bent only under snow.
Would the flowers in the spring wind be always lovely?
When the cold wind and snow blow, you will envy my lot.

The sijo, however, does not specialize just in the love sentiment or one's unbending loyalty to the king. Because the new genre, though mysteriously, was started by neo-Confucian scholars, the poems were bound to express their ethical code, and because it was adopted later by the common people it eventually became the people's literature. *Chung-gu Young-on*, one of the oldest anthologies of sijo poems, has 38 pieces on the theme of separation, 28 on leisurely life, 22 on the regrets of life, 11 on drinking, and 12 on the loyalty to the king.

The range of themes in the anthology represents the typical concern of sijo poets. Although the first poets of sijo wrote on their Confucian codes of life such as loyalty to the king, filial piety to parents, and friendship to neighbours, the genre gradually absorbed all the sentiments that prevailed in the minds of the people. The sijo poems, therefore, are full of works on themes of Taoistic thoughts like the love of nature and the resignation of worldly cares. Indeed, there are great numbers of poems on drinking and leisurely life, which often give the impression of being decadent. This, combined with the poems on the indulgence in love, certainly reflects the feelings of the common people of the 18th and 19th centuries.

Perhaps this earned the nomenclature of sijo, which meant the songs of the time, i.e. popular songs as against learned poetry in Chinese. It is not known what the new genre was called when it had first started, but by the 18th century the name of musical nature was given. The other designations also indicated the musical character of sijo; it was sometimes called the sinjo, the new song or the song of the East; sometimes it was called the sinkok, the new melody; and sometimes it was called the sinsung, the new voice. All these appelations invariably suggested that the sijo in fact was a musical device. The words are poetry, and the genre abounds with poetic devices. But the sijo was adopted and appreciated among the people as songs rather than poetry. (Even nowadays the singing of sijo poems is popular.) Depending upon how it was sung it again had different names. When it was sung without much dramatic stress, it was the pyong sijo (pyong meaning flat); when the stress was on the middle line it was called jong-ori sijo; when the first line was sung with the highest pitch, it was called the jirom sijo.

Even the arrangement of syllables denotes its musical

design. Its strict control of syllables in each line seems to have been planned for the maximum rhythmic effect. The first line has 12 syllables, dividing them into four units of 3, 4, 3, 4; the second line again has 12 syllables, and once again they are divided into four units of 3, 4, 3, 4. The last line observes the same four divisional structure, but has 15 syllables, which are divided into 3, 5, 4, 3. There are some slight variations in the total number of syllables or characters, and also in the division of syllables. The first line can go in 3, 4, 4, 4 or 3, 5, 3, 4, the second line in 3, 3, 3, 4 or 3, 4, 4, 4 and the last line in 3, 3, 4, 4, 3 or 3, 3, 4, 5. All these variations do not allow a sequence in principle to go beyond the total of 45 or 46 syllables, though this rule again can have exceptions. Because of this rigidity on the number of syllables, the ending of the last line sometimes concludes in a rather unfinished way. When the poet has used up all his allowance of syllables, he suddenly ends his last line without a proper verb. (In a Korean sentence the verb comes last.)

A solution for this limitation was the creation of the sasul sijo in the 17th or the 18th century when the genre became very popular among the people. The rise of the sasul sijo is not attributed to any specific author. As a large volume of sijo poems are written by anonymous writers, the sasul sijo, which represents the 'common' feeling of the common people most comprehensibly, often does not claim any specified authors. The sasul sijo in this sense is the most typical folk literature of the Yi Dynasty.

The sasul sijo in its effort to accommodate the common sentiment of the people started in the spirit of prose narrative. While the sijo poems proper were composed in a strictly poetic form, the sasul sijo broke the tight rule on the number of syllables and on the three line structure. The middle line became prosaic and lengthy and later the three line format adopted the three stanza structure. Chung Cheol's 'Drinking Song', a rare expression to be written by a specific individual author, is a good example of sasul sijo:

Let's have a drink; let's have another.
Let's pick flowers and count the endless drinks with flower-petals.

Once dead we will be taken away in a carrier tied in a straw mat.
Or carried in a grand bier, mourned by ten thousand people.
Once in the woods of eulalia, reeds, oaks and poplars
Under a yellow sun, a white moon,
In the fine rain, the heavy snow, or the whirlwind,
Who would ask us to share drinks?
What's the use of regretting when monkeys whistle on our graves?

Although the sasul sijo was an attempt to take poetry away from the sijo and replace it with narrative elements, it remained as poetry, abiding within the regulations of poetry. It has musical designs and also control on the number of syllables, though flexible and loose. It was sung as a song. But it was a song to be enjoyed as much in its melodies as in its message.

The sijo, however, when it was sung, had rather monotonous tunes. What is more, each sijo did not have its own tune. All the sijo poems were sung more or less in the same tune. After listening to half a dozen of them, the remaining ones sound the same. What distinguishes one poem from another is the message it carries and how it is presented. The popularity of a poem largely depended on its theme, its use of images, its choice of words, and its musicality. The sijo, in other words, is a combination of poetry and music.

It is this combination that made the sijo popular with the people. It appealed to their poetic sense with its aesthetic beauty, and to their ear with its musical effect. While the poetry in Chinese insisted on being the high art and kept distance from the popular taste, the sijo moved closer and closer to the heart of the people. The vernacular language, the intimate expressions, the popular themes, the fresh, daring images and the pleasing rhythmic beat, all these contributed to making the indigenous tradition a truly national literature.

It is a great pity that this rich tradition (the present surviving works amount to roughly 3,500 poems) suffered from the decline of the Yi Dynasty at the end of the 19th century and was completely stopped during the Japanese Occupation of 1919–1945. After World War II and the Korean

War of 1950–53, there has emerged a nationwide movement to revive the national literature which has produced some good *sijo* poets, but it will take a considerable time before it catches up with the old spirit and gets into another phase of enlivening development of its old tradition. However, the sijo is deeply rooted in the heart of the Korean people and in due course the old roots will send out shoots and flowers.

30 Sijo Poems

TRANSLATED BY CHUNG CHONG-WHA

Everybody has a lively mouth;
He forgets his faults and abuses others.
Don't speak ill of others; try to reform yourself.

ANONYMOUS

Rafters may be short or long; pillars tilted or
twisted.
Do not laugh at my shabby cottage.
The full moon shining on tangled grass is mine.

SHIN HUM

Shin Hum (1566–1628) served as the minister of home affairs under King Sunjo (1567–1608), becoming the prime minister in 1627 under King Injo (1623–1649). When King Kwanghae succeeded the throne he was exiled briefly, but reinstated by King Injo, becoming the minister of general affairs. He left 30 volumes of essays and poems.

Weeds in a swamp have grown tall in the spring rain.
How so envious that they do not have any worries.
We are less than grass and full of worries.

YI JUNG-HWAN

Yi Jung-hwan passed his first government civil service examination in 1633, but in 1636 he decided not to seek his government career when he saw the Chinese invasion (1636–37) and the country subsequently subjugated by the Ching Dynasty. He is supposed to have left ten sijo poems during this period. When his parents died he stayed near the grave for six years, barely eating. This examplary life of Confucian filial piety moved King Hyongjong (1659–1674), and he was awarded the title of *Jipyong*, a royal inspector attached to the Justice Department.

Though the colour of cloud is said nice, it easily turns black.
Though the sound of the wind clear, it often ceases to stir.
That which is nice and ceaseless is water.

YUN SUN-DO

Yun Sun-do (1587–1671) was one of the leading *sijo* poets of the Yi Dynasty. He served as the Deputy Lord Mayor of Seoul and the magistrate of Sungju County. His straightforward character made many enemies in the government and he was in political exile twice.

Why on earth do the flowers wither as soon as they bloom?
Why on earth does grass fade as soon as it becomes green?
Perhaps what is changeless must be the rock.

YUN SUN-DO

The green willows may have a thousand branches,
but they cannot tie up the passing spring wind.
Bees and butterflies may enjoy flowers, but they
cannot stop them from falling.
Important though the root may be, you cannot stop
him from going.

YI WON-IK

Yi Won-ik (1547–1634) served King Sunjo as his prime minister during and after the Hideyoshi invasion. Although he was exiled briefly by King Kwanghae, he was soon called back to his premiership.

That the clouds never think is completely untrue.
They float in the mid-sky and move round at will.
They follow the sun and cover it on a bright day.

YI JON-O

Yi Jon-o (1341–1371) first passed the civil service examination in 1360 and soon became a government historian. When Monk Shin Don became deeply involved in the running of government affairs, he publicly warned against him, and subsequently he was expelled from his central government post. He died at the age of thirty and was awarded the posthumous title of the President of the National Academy.

I've forgotten fame; also wealth and glory.
I've forgotten all the cares and worries of the world.
As I've forgotten even myself, others would forget me
too.

KIM KWANG-WOOK

Kim Kwang-wook (1580–1656) started his government career in his early twenties and served as vice minister of justice, the Lord Mayor of Seoul, the Governor of Kyunggi Province, and later deputy prime minister. In 1615 he was exiled by King Kwanghae for ten years. He left a book of sijo poems, *Yulli Yulgok*.

Even the sun returns to the mountain and river when the day's gone.
Even the moon becomes smaller after the mid-month.
I think fame and wealth are no exceptions.

ANONYMOUS

Glory is false; wealth is a dream.
When the funeral bells cease ringing in the mountain
grave yard,
Sorrow and remorse have no way of reaching back.

KIM SOOJANG

Kim Soojang (1690–?) is, along with Kim Chun-taik, one of the two major poets of the 18th century. Though he held only a clerical position in his social career, he left behind an important book of sijo poems, *Haedong-gayo* (the Songs of the East), which he published in 1763.

Let's have a drink; let's have another.
Let's pick flowers and count the endless drinks with flower-petals.
Once dead we will be taken away in a carrier tied in a straw mat;
Or carried in a grand bier, mourned by ten thousand people.
Once in the wood of eulalia, reeds, oaks and poplars,
Under a yellow sun, a white moon,
In the fine rain, the heavy snow, or the whirlwind,
Who would ask us to share drinks?
What's use of regretting when monkeys whistle on our graves?

CHUNG CHEOL

Chung Cheol (1536–1593) is one of the great poets of the Yi Dynasty. His *Song-gang-gasa* (Songs of *Song-gang*) is a unique achievement in the field of sijo. Unlike Yun Sun-do, the other great master of sijo poetry, Chung Cheol tends to moralize in his poetry reflecting a strong Confucian element. However, this poem represents another trait of the poet, in which he indulges in drinking and the life in nature, renouncing worldly cares.

He was heavily involved in the disputes of political sectionism, he himself acting as the boss of *Suh-in* (the Western Party) as against *Dong-in* (the Eastern Party). At the height of his career he served King Sunjo (1567–1608) in the capacity of minister for general affairs and later of ambassador to China.

The moon is so bright and clear; I ride a boat on an autumn river.
Water flows under the sky and the moon floats on it.
Boatman, fish the moon, I want to drink with it.

PARK SANG

Park Sang's life is unknown except that he wrote this poem.

Having retired from the worldly successes
I've built a house in the forest
With a library of ten thousand books.
Servants are ploughing the field,
Falcons are trained for hunting,
Stallions are saddled,
And wine barrels are filled.
A beauty is called to my side
To sing Shun*'s 'South Wind Ode'*
To a paulonia harp.
While drunken, I lie in peace.
What else do I want in life but this?

ANONYMOUS

Your promise to my eyes; you have finally bloomed.
Under the moon in the dusk, even shadows look thin.
Clear fragrance floats in the glass; I want to get drunk.

AN MIN-YOUNG

This is a series of An's Plum Blossom Songs which he composed in 1840 when he went to a party at Park Hyo Kwan's mountain villa in company of friends and *kisaeng* girls.

An Min-young was a minstrel in the time of King Heunjong (1834–1849) and King Chuljong (1848–1863). He edited the historical *Kagok Wonryu*, anthology of *sijo* poems.

Lady, don't be so proud; do not boast your beauty.
Have you not seen the wild chrysanthemums on the
hills behind your house?
Once the late autumn frost hits them, they become
nothing but fuel wood.

ANONYMOUS

I wish I could cut out the waist of this deep mid-
winter night
And curl it softly, softly under the warm spring quilt;
And slowly, slowly spread it on the night my love
comes back.

HWANG JINIE

Hwang Jinie (?–1544) is one of the best *sijo* poets of the Yi Dynasty. She belonged, unfortunately, to the humble class of *kisaeng*, the professional hostesses trained to entertain gentlemen with songs and dances, and often poetry as well. She is reputed to be a great beauty and to have seduced many great scholars and politicians of her time, but her poem reflects a woman's lonely heart.

I cannot forget the man I had last night.
Was he a tile-maker's son? He was good at kneading clay.
Was he a mole cub? He was good at digging.
Was he a boatman's son? He was good at rowing.
I've not had all these before; I feel funny even now.
I have had countless men, but I swear I will not forget the man I had last night.

YI JUNBO

Yi Jungbo (1693–1766) is one of the poets whose work luckily has survived. 78 poems are included in Chung Byungwook's *Sijo Moonhak Sajon* (An Anthology of Sijo Literature). He served King Yungjo as Minister of Culture.

Lady, heat for sale! The early summer heat for sale!
The late summer heat for sale!
The heat of many summers and winters for sale!

The mid-summer night heat that burnt my whole intestines
And made me pant and sweat on a moonlit bed
While legs and arms entangled; that is for sale!
The long mid-winter night heat that burnt my throat
And made me drink the cold rice water in one gulp
After two bodies had become one in a thick quilt in a warm room,
And had become almost out of breath; that is also for sale, Lady!

Dear man, among your goods, who would refuse the two love heats?
Please, don't sell it to others. Let me buy them.

ANONYMOUS

Che *is a great country;* Cho *also a big country.*
A small country of Ding *is squeezed between the two powers.*
Well, leave it. I will serve both Che *and* Cho.

SO CHOON-POONG

So Choon-poong was a *kisaeng* girl in the Yi Dynasty and left three sijo poems behind, but her biographical facts are unknown. This poem seems to reveal her position being squeezed by two contending lovers.

I had a good dream last night; today I have a letter
from my beloved.
I read it a hundred times over and then fell asleep;
with the letter on my chest.
Though it was not so heavy, my heart was ever so
pressed.

ANONYMOUS

Separation has become fire and burns my heart.
Tears have become rain and almost put them out.
Alas, sighs have become the wind and the fire is
renewed.

ANONYMOUS

The moon rose on the top of pine tree and sank at the end of turf.
A harp across my lap, I am seated alone on the rock.
I hear a single goose flying crying.

ANONYMOUS

Spring is back in the countryside: I've got so much to do.
I mend the net and the boy ploughs the field.
When would I be able to cut the stemming herbs in the hills behind?

HWANG HEE

Hwang Hee (1363–1452) was one of the most renowned statesmen of the early Yi Dynasty. He started his civil service career in the last phase of the Koryo Dynasty, but rose to the higher government positions in the new dynasty. He served in turn as the minister of the whole six government ministries and subsequently became the prime minister under King Sejong. He is reputed to be one of the most exemplary civil servants of the Yi Dynasty, being modest, honest and generous. He made a great contribution to the reformation of the government system and the general customs of the nation.

The old sage hasn't seen me; nor I him.
Though we haven't met I've his way before me.
While his path is before, what else can I do but
follow it?

YI HWANG

Yi Hwang (1501–1570), better known as Toe-gye for his philosophy of neo-Confucianism, is the greatest scholar of the Yi Dynasty. Yi Hwang served in the government roughly between 1534 and 1555 as a local magistrate, the vice minister of justice, and the president of the National Academy, but in later years he devoted his life to scholarship at his Dosan Academy in Andong.

I would like to cut out the lights of autumn sky that
appear after rain;
Make a suit of them with silver needle of five-colour
threads,
And send it to my lord in the nine gate palace.

ANONYMOUS

Do not laugh at the pine; it is bent only under snow.
Would the flowers in the spring wind be always
lovely?
When the cold wind and snow blow, you will envy
my lot.

CHOI YOUNG

Choi Young (1316–1388) was one of the great generals who tried to revitalize the ailing Koryo Dynasty. When his plan of invading Ming and recovering Manchuria failed as a result of the revolution by Yi Sung-gye, Choi was sent into exile and subsequently assassinated. This poem seems to mock at Yi Sung-gye's rising fortune while Choi's star was waning.

Who calls the bamboo bent that bends under the
snow?
If it were bent, would it be green in the white?
You are the only one who keeps up in the coldest
winter days.

WON CHUN-SUK

Won Chun-suk refused to serve the new regime when the Koryo Dynasty was overthrown by Yi Sung-gye. There were many invitations from the kings of the new Dynasty, but he declined all of them. This poem, which is one of the two surviving works (he is reputed to have written two books of poems), reflects his loyalty to the old dynasty.

You heron, don't laugh at a crow being so black.
It may be dark outside, but it may not be so inside.
Perhaps you're the only one that is white outside and
black inside.

YI JICK

Yi Jick (1362–1431) first started his career in the last phase of the Koryo Dynasty. When Yi Sungge led a coup d'état and founded the Yi Dynasty he held many important key posts and later became the prime minister.

This poem seems to refer to the political situation he is thrown into; he seems to refer himself as a crow, traditionally a bird of ill omen. The heron must be his political opponents who remained loyal to the dying dynasty.

A crow is covered with snow and looks whitish black.
Can the full moon be dark at night?
My red-heart loyalty to the Lord would never change.

PARK PAENG-NYON

Park Paeng-nyon (1417–1456) was one of the scholars who helped King Sejong invent the Korean alphabet. He later served as the governor of Choongchung Province and the vice minister of justice. When King Sejo overthrew his nephew, King Danjong, Park sided with the deposed king. He was arrested for his plot to oust the usurped king and was tortured to death. This poem is believed to be the pronouncement of his loyalty to the rightful king.

Who did that candle outside window part company
with?
Shedding tears outside, does it realize it's singeing
inside?
We are like the candle; we don't know the heart is
ablaze.

YI GAE

Yi Gae (1417–1456), one of the Six Martyrs, served under King Sejong and became an active member in the creation of the Korean alphabet. When King Danjong usurped the crown, he plotted to reinstate the legitimate king, but he was arrested and tortured to death.

What would I become after this life?
I would become the tallest pine tree on the peak of
Mount Pong Lai,
And shine out my greenness when the snow buries
the whole world.

SUNG SAM-MOON

Sung Sam-moon (1418–1456) was a scholar in the time of King Sejong (1418–1450) and played an important role in the creation of *Hangul*, the Korean alphabet. When King Danjong (1452–1455) was thrown out by his uncle, later King Sejo (1455–1468), Sung stood firm against the new king and tried with the other Six Martyrs to reinstate the legitimate king. But his secret move was betrayed; he was arrested and tortured to death. This poem is said to have been composed to the new king's attempt to change his loyalty to the deposed.

Two Early Poems and 'Words from the Heart'

The Song of Yellow Birds

KING YURI

Yellow birds play around
Male and female together,
How painful that I'm alone.
Who do I return with?

translated by Chung Chong-wha

The poem is ascribed to King Yuri (19BC–AD18) of the Kingdom of Kokuryo. It is believed to be the very first Korean poem written in Chinese and recorded in the history of Korean literature. The King, who lost his first wife, remarried two Chinese sisters but the younger returned home because of her elder sister's jealousy. He composed this poem to show his grief. A pair of courting warblers on a tree seem to have inspired this sad poem.

The Song of *Cho-Yong*

CHO-YONG

Under the bright moonlight in the capital city
I caroused late at night.
When I returned to my chamber
Lo, there are four legs in my bed!

Two were mine;
Whose legs are the other two?
Even though the two were mine once
What can I do when they are taken away?

translated by Chung Chong-wha

Cho-Yong is reputed to be one of the seven sons of the Dragon King. In 899 King Hun-gang of the Kingdom of Silla and his royal entourage encountered the Dragon King and his sons near the sea at Gaiwonto, a village near Ulsan. They began to dance and sing for the King, who took one son, Cho-Yong, to the Palace. Cho-Yong became very popular for his musical talents in the capital city. Later he married a princess and lived happily. One night he returned home late and found his wife in bed with a man, supposedly the demon of pestilence. Instead of making a scene he left his house and sang this song. Since then people sing this song whenever there is an epidemic in their village.

Words From the Heart

(Simo Sa)
by an unknown poet

Alas! I am sad!
Let me tell you all my sadness.

Human life, if lived to the full,
Is barely a hundred years,
And out of that there are the nights,
And the time spent in sleep is immeasurable.
Splitting a hundred years in two,
One sleeps for fifty years,
And sad and happy times
Split again into halves.
So if one lives all the hundred years
That is a little more than twenty years,
The time one has lived is a matter of grief.

In that time, with good fortune,
If one gets riches and honour, recognition and fame,
Bottom or top class graduate, first on the list, Doctor of Letters,
Diarist, Recorder, Third Minister, Second Minister,
County Magistrate, Town or City Magistrate,
City Governor or Capital Magistrate, Provincial Governor or Army Commander.
Recognition and fame are splendid
And riches and honour complement them.
The king treats him well
And the common people respect him.
So the glorious fame of his lifetime
After his death for ever and ever
Shines in the Annals.
This is how one has an unbroken line of descendants,
So if that man is praised

Down for hundreds and thousands of years,
However dead he may be,
Though dead, he is alive.
If he was like that when he was alive,
When he is said to be dead, can it be a matter of grief?

When Heaven produces men,
Their fortunes are all different.
So one with a farmer's cape and wielding a hoe,
Wearing a farmer's trousers,
And, on rainy days and fine days alike,
Having his fingernails and toenails torn off,
All his meagre fortune on an 'A' frame,[1]
Sweat soaking the jacket on his back,
Higher and higher
Climbs over the high mountains and steep passes.
One with a tassel threaded on a bamboo hat,
And wrapped up old rags,
When the blizzard strikes the pillars,
Addresses himself to another's house.
In his bamboo hat and with an old sack,
Begging his food, the Sŏn[2] priest
Twists up his intestines
And loses hope in Amitābha.
Such creatures
Should not be produced.
For a just God
It is an unfair fortune.
If he disappears and dies
Not having seen a happy world,
In what place shall we find
The traces of what he has bequeathed to mankind?
For such poor wretches
We discard as soon as possible.

Alas! My friend!
It was that friend's fortune.
In the house left to him by his ancestors
His family fortune was good enough,
And he was a fine tall figure of a man,
Extraordinarily well built.

He set his mind on recognition and fame
And ran out into the world,
And though one may count off each and every one
Of the travellers who have returned through the Gate,
For talent possessed, of old and now,
There has been none better,
But wherever he went, he was followed,
As by the horse of the Tongp'a Station,
So he could not cheat his fate
And had to return.
He had his pavilion high above the boundary wall,
Thatch-roofed, neat and tidy,
And he ate nine times a month, lived ten years without
  change,
Swept away every thought of it from his mind,
And rivers and lakes, nature became his companions,
And he plighted his troth to them for ever.
So, when the full-ripened rice came to ear,
Spade and plough were cast aside
And he cast his fishing rod
At barbel and gudgeon.
'You gentlemen who seek recognition and fame
Buried in the dust,
Your anxieties are unknown to me.
Can you know the fun I have,
Until my knees are higher than my ears
And my strong hairs turn yellow
Enjoying without regret
All the years which Heaven has given me,
Seeing my son's children and my daughter's children,
And their grandchildren and their grandchildren's children
  filling my house?'

Such good fortune
As no one else had, he hoped for,
But perhaps the spirits were jealous
Or creation had gone wild at his birth,
Because the dew formed in the morning
Hangs on the tip of the grass,
Until a wild wind puffs,
When, helpless, it vanishes.

Even saints like Confucius and Mencius
And strong men such as Pen and Yü
Cannot avoid dying in the end,
And become eternal dust.
They are dead, it is said, but is there only sadness?
This death is the saddest of all.
The universe's time, which flies by,
Flashes like the spark from a stone,
And the things humans will do so furiously
Must surely pass away like a dream.

The talent which he possessed all his life
He did not use even once,
Then he was tied and bound with hemp from the Six Towns
And buried deep in wood,
And he even when the silver nails were hammered in
He knew no urgency,
So if one offers him in all sincerity
Jujubes, chestnuts and a glass of wine,
He has fallen into a deep sleep
And when he will wake up is uncertain.
When he set off on the right day
To an auspicious spot in the green hills,
I said my farewells at the shrine,
And turned back, leaving no trace,
And the dirge trailed on
And the handbells tinkled.
Not only I, but the others too,
Shed all their sad tears,
Where is he going?
Let me ask him where he is going.
If you meet your parents
On the road you have gone on this time,
I would be glad
Because of the yearning which they had for you when they departed,
But your wife, sons, daughters, daughters-in-law,
Who will they rely on?
You are so indifferent to them
That you have not one word of regard for them.
If you are in your ancestral tomb,

Might they not reprove you?
The empty mountain is deserted
And a cuckoo calls.
After they have put him in the black wood coffin,
They slide the lid across the deep grave,
And on top of the emaciated breast
They pile, pile, pile the earth
And with a great big rammer
Ram it up with steady strokes,
So I think my human thoughts,
'Can they bear to do that?'
But after one is gone
One wishes to be buried deep,
However much they may search
For traces that he has been in the world,
Will he have left even a shadow
But returned with it?
The whole huge body of a man
Must surely become a handful of earth.

They made up a beautiful memorial tablet,
A piece of chestnut wood, one foot two inches,
And, whether it was there or not,
Called upon his soul,
And took it in comfort upon the little palanquin
And returned it to his former home.
The adults of the family went out,
And then, as they came in to before the gate,
Even the dogs, animals, barked when they saw him
In welcome,
But his appearance
Is so sad
That there is only the sound of lamentation
As they call upon heaven and earth.
Now it is no use,
No use at all.
Helpless was even the splendid majesty
Of the First Emperor of Ch'in and Emperor Wu of Han.
Useless was the wealth amassed
In the T'ao-chu store by Chih Chu'ung.
P'eng-lai-shan, wherever it may be,

Has the elixir of life,
But that was the blessed fate
Of An Ch'isheng and Ch'ih Sung-tzu.
Can they have had for hundreds of years
Their black hair and their children's faces?
I beg you, you fairies,
Give me one bag of the elixir.
To my poor friend
I shall give one pill and restore him to life —
A hundred years is short, you may say,
But I shall give him life again,
So the things he could not do in his lifetime
We shall do them all, however trivial,
And all the friends who were close to him through his life
Wish to gather again and enjoy themselves.

Alas! I am sad!
There is no end to my sadness.
At the gateway a lone goose
With both wings drooping
Cries at the loss of his mate.
His long cry is sad.
It is a night when the moon is bright
On the River Hsiao-hsiang and Lake Tung-t'ing.

Alas! I am sad!
Enough of my sadness!
Lay aside this sorrow!
I'll coil it up, coil by coil, I'll put it in a wine cup
And drink one cup, two cups, hundreds and thousands of
cups,
I'll drink and drink, and I'll never sober up, I think.*

translated by W.E. Skillend

* Notes

1 A-frame: is a back pack made of two pieces set as in the letter A with cross braces to hold them. A base is attached near the bottom to create a shelf on which to place the load. The carrier always carries a typical notched walking stick, the notch of which fits into the cross piece of the A forming a tripod to hold the load upright when he stops to rest, or to hold the pack in position while it is being loaded.

2 Sŏon priest: Zen priest.

19th Century Books with Stories in Korean

W.E. SKILLEND

We think that there is something typically and timelessly Korean about the relationship between the people in that story, a humaneness in people's attitudes to each other, an attempt to get along together happily somehow in a very difficult world. We hope that the story simply gave pleasure in the reading, but we would like now to turn to the perhaps academic, but we think important question of placing it in its context. For, though it is a typical Korean story in its way, it is not actually typical of the stories which we find in the couple of hundred books containing stories in Korean which we can still find from the 19th century.

What we would like to do, ideally, would be to trace the development of story-telling in Korean from the simple, orally transmitted tale, which Korea has like any other country, to the modern novel, but we must admit that that would not be easy. The task is immensely complicated by the fact that several very enthusiastic and convincing accounts of the history, or pre-history, of the novel were written by Koreans before the material for compiling such a history had been properly evaluated, indeed before it was even known that such materials existed.

Such accounts go back to that given in the 1930s by Kim T'aejun in the several editions of his 'History of the Korean Novel'. We mention this because, although our view of this subject given here, in full awareness of the limitations on our own knowledge, is highly personal, even idiosyncratic, we feel that accounts by others which go back essentially to the work of Kim T'aejun, cannot now be substantiated.

Kim T'aejun, for instance, began his history of the Korean novel with the writing of 'The Story of Hong Kiltong' by Hŏ Kyun in the early years of the 17th century. We simply cannot accept that now, since the only works of that title which we have are patently late 19th century works, and the evidence that Hŏ Kyun wrote any work of that title is very thin. Kim T'aejun placed later in the 17th century a novel called 'Records of the Year of the Red Rat', that is 1636, the date of the invasion of Korea by the Manchu, but, as far as we can ascertain, it seems to be pure fiction that any novel of such a title ever existed. There is a novel entitled 'The Story of the Lady Pak' which contains a story of those wars, and which Kim T'aejun also placed as a 17th century novel, but there can be no question at all that that novel belongs to the very last decade of the 19th century.

The next landmark in this history is the writings of Kim Manjung at the end of the 17th century, and we shall try to see those writings in context shortly, but the 18th century poses problems. Kim T'aejun filled it with novels derived from oral traditions and portrayed it as the period when the traditional Korean novel reached its peak, with a decline in the 19th century. The basic objection to this theory is that we do not have a single novel, a single actual book, that is, which can be dated as 18th century. All our material in fact dates from the 19th century except for that which can be clearly dated as 20th century. So, let us look at this material, thanking Kim T'aejun for the many insights which he was the first to give into the quality of traditional stories in Korean, but bidding farewell to his historical account of the development of the novel.

The most striking group of texts of novels in Korean that we can now see are the hundred or so novels in over two thousand volumes which are preserved from the ladies' quarters of the old royal palace in Seoul. These are impressive, some of them remarkably so. There is a series of three novels, for instance, in 235 volumes in all — that would come out as some 50 hefty volumes in English translation — telling a continuous story of several related families over several generations, involving hundreds of characters in thousands of episodes, yet consistent in style and plot. The late Professor Chŏng Pyŏnguk worked on this story in his final years, and, for all his lifetime's experience of Korean classical literature, was overwhelmed by the talents he saw in its unidentified author. Yet what must strike the literary historian is that, not only does it appear to be impossible to identify the author even in the most general terms, but besides that we cannot even find any evidence that anyone had ever read this novel before Professor Chŏng Pyŏnguk. In what sense, then, do we call it 'Korean Literature'? What in Korean culture formed the author of such a work? How did his (or her?) work help form subsequent writers? Indeed, when was the work composed? None of these questions can yet be answered, and in particular the date of the work may be anywhere between 1800 and 1900.

This might be as good a point as any to look a little more closely at Kim Manjung, an important writer of works in literary Chinese, who lived from 1637 to 1692. It is currently felt, and we share the feeling, that the tradition in his family that he wrote two very good novels in Korean is reliable. One was 'The Nine Cloud Dream', which one can enjoy in Richard Rutt's translation in a book called 'Virtuous Women', published in 1974, and the other was 'The Wanderings of the Lady Hsieh in the South', which unfortunately has not yet been translated. The first is a most delicately contrived fantasy, in which, within a frame of Buddhist mysticism, the hero is portrayed as enjoying a full, satisfying life of material well-being. The second is more subtly contrived, a remarkable allegory on late 17th century politics. While it would be perverse to refuse to accept these works as masterpieces of the late 17th century, it is an unfortunate fact that we can read them now only in translations into literary Chinese which were made in the early years of the 18th century and in translations then back into Korean which were made in the 19th century. Furthermore, Kim Manjung himself is an oasis in a vast desert. He tells us that he enjoyed some 17th century Korean poetry, but we have no knowledge at all of any author of Korean prose before him, unless two works of palace memoires which we shall mention shortly, were actually available for him to read, nor can we find any writer of prose for at least a hundred years after his death. As with the authors of the palace novels two hundred years later, where did Kim Manjung as a novelist come from, and where did he go to? Can we see him, as a novelist, through translations into Korean of his works translated into Chinese?

If we look at the novels which we do have from the 19th century, and suppose that these may derive from 18th century or earlier originals, we are still left with a problem: that none of these seem to approach within a million miles of 'The Nine Cloud Dream' or 'The Wanderings of the Lady Hsieh in the South' as novels in concept. It is possible that the inspiration to create this thing called 'a novel' came from the reading of novels in Chinese, and indeed by the end of the 19th century all Chinese novels which had a level of morality acceptable in Korean society seem to have been translated into Korean, but the most popular by far were the blood and thunder tales from the inter-dynastic warring periods of Chinese history, especially those from the Three Kingdoms period which were so popular in China from Yüan, and still are today, as much in Korea as in China.

In this connection, westerners must be confused by what they would see as a failure in Korea to distinguish at all clearly between history as such and historical fiction. The importance attached to history in Korea, as in China, is enormous, but it is not always history as we might see it. Even official Korean histories seem to us to place too much reliance on the apocryphal anecdote with an important moral lesson to teach posterity, and some historical novels are little more than direct translations of what purport to be historical documents, such as memoirs. From the end of the 19th century in Korea we find many popular tales set in the wars of Imjin and Pyŏongja, the year of the black dragon, 1596, the date of the Japanese invasion of Korea, and the year of the red rat, 1636, the date of the Manchu invasion. As another 'black dragon' year, 1896, saw the return of Japanese troops to Korea, the production of such stories was obviously stimulated, and the heroes of three hundred years earlier, such as the Grand Master Samyŏngdang, who had mastered both the magical and the military arts in his temple retreats, had a very clear role to play as the Japanese came to annex Korea for the first half of the 20th century.

There is another small group of works which pose the same problem of distinguishing history from fiction, essentially three supposed palace memoires. The one of these which relates to the earliest period is entitled 'Diary of the Year of the Black Ox', that is 1613, which covers the period 1602 to 1621, a very turbulent period in palace politics. Although majority opinion in Korean scholarship seems to be that this is an historical novel in diary form, of uncertain date, it is uninteresting enough in style and difficult enough in language for us to allow that it is at least derived from an actual diary of the time.

The second work appears under such titles as 'The True History of Queen Inhyŏn', and one version of this may be read in English translation, again, in 'Virtuous Women'. It was Queen Inhyŏn who was at the centre of the political controversy of the 1690s which is treated allegorically in Kim Manjung's 'Lady Hsieh' novel, and it is difficult to see it as pure coincidence that the first written suggestion that that novel was a political allegory, the publication of the Korean translation of the novel, and the date of one of the texts of the 'Queen Inhyŏn' story are all in 1851–1852. Somewhere, in all these facts, there is a good story to be written, we feel, though we are certainly not able to do it ourselves yet.

Finally there is the striking story to be found in texts which have titles like *Hanjung nok*. These are written as the autobiography of 'the Lady Hong of the Hyegyŏng Palace', and tell the tragic story of her husband, who is most popularly known by Koreans as 'Crown Prince Sado'. Several English translations of this moving work have been made, but we know of only two that have been published, by Bruce K. Grant and Kim Chin-man in 1980, with the translation of the title 'Reminiscences in Retirement' as a sub-title, and by Mrs Yang Hee Choe Wall under the title of *Memoirs of a Korean Queen*. The problem with this work is that none of the texts of it can be confidently dated as earlier than the first years of the 20th century, a hundred years later than the events described, and again one cannot help noting that Crown Prince Sado was posthumously elevated to the rank of king, and the Lady Hong to the rank of queen in 1899. Again we hesitate to ascribe any importance to this fact for the history of the novel in Korean, but we cannot help wondering.

These three palace stories all existed only in manuscript until they were printed very recently, and all the novels in the ladies' quarters of the former royal palace are also manuscript copies. Those in the former palace are most beautifully written and bound, and we can also find a few dozen other stories in manuscripts which can be identified as belonging to households related to the royal family. In all these cases it is striking that it is extremely rare to find other texts of the same stories, as if the palace and each related household each had its own stock of stories which it shared with no one else, again raising the question of what exactly we mean when we call these works of 'Korean literature'. How many Koreans, we must ask, wrote or even read works such as these? And over what period? It is very difficult to date any of them as earlier than the second half of the 19th century.

From the same period, and from later, indeed even from the second quarter of the 20th century, we can find many manuscripts of poorer quality, some of them identified as the property of lending libraries. Again, however, exactly how much of a role these lending libraries played in the spread of the habit of reading novels is not known. It would seem, at first sight, that the existence of printed versions of novels in 19th century Korea might be an indication that a wider access to such literature might have been opened at that time. We can now read about 70 such printed novels, but our knowledge of these has come about in a rather curious way.

Korea was unbelievably isolated from the rest of the world until the 1870s. Among the foreigners who tried to discover more about this unknown land, some tried to learn its language. Many tried to learn to speak Korean in order to preach the Christian gospel to Koreans, and some of those who did so before the 1860s were beheaded for their unprovoked intrusion. One or two, however, took a more cautious approach to the Korean language at a safe distance through its literautre. One novel, 'The Story of Yim Kyŏngsŏp', for instance, was published as a language text book by the Japanese Foreign Office in 1881. In the same year an English diplomat in Japan, W.G. Aston, was learning the language by studying some 25 novels which he had got a Korean acquaintance to bring him from Seoul. All these were printed books, very similar in appearance to the Japanese novels which Aston had also been reading. He preserved his Korean books very carefully, but, by some quirk of fate, they all ended up being purchased for the Czar of Russia, and they subsequently lay in Leningrad almost unknown to the outside world until a catalogue of them in Russian was published in 1963.

In 1890, by which time Korea had had regular diplomatic relations with most western countries for nearly a decade, Maurice Courant, who worked at the French Embassy, began his monumental bibliographical studies, opening up a whole new world of literature and printing to the west. Almost all the couple of thousand works which Courant described were in literary Chinese, but Courant did master the Korean language to a degree that few foreigners were to achieve until 60 years later. He seemed destined to become the first professor of Korean in Europe, in Paris, and one of his colleagues at the embassy, a Mr Colin de Plancy, had printings made to order of all the novels which could be found in print at the time. They were about 50 in number, and these were nicely bound and donated to the College of Living Oriental Languages in Paris to await the coming boom in the study of Korean. Unfortunately, the university professors in Paris refused to see in Courant, a provincial who demeaned himself by talking in Chinese with Chinese lay-abouts in France, professorial material, and the project never came to fruition. Like Aston's books in Leningrad, Colin de Plancy's books were destined to lie neglected for 70 years.

Courant also recorded that a German diplomat, G. von der Gabelentz, made a large collection of printed novels in Korean, but there is no record of his collection ever having been used for any practical purpose, and it was sadly lost in the final days of the Second World War. However, the British Museum did manage to pick up in Berlin another collection of 25 printed novels in Korean, and then to keep them safe from public view until the middle of the 20th century.

It is necessary to go into this apparent digression from the history of Korean literature because it is a strange fact that very few of these printed texts of novels survived in Korea itself, and, without Courant's careful recording of the facts, we might have had considerable difficulty in deciding how old those few texts surviving in Korea are. While such scholarship as there was in Korea on this subject remained isolated, under the Japanese occupation, from the materials and slight scholarly interest in them in the west, they were simply 'old books', and no one had any idea of how old 'old' was. Kim T'aejun was certainly able to accept them as being two or three times as old as they really were. However, scholarship since the 1960s has given us a clearer picture now of the publishing trade, if it may be so designated, in 19th century Korea.

It is now clear that the printing of novels in Korean from engraved wood blocks was an activity essentially of the 1850s to the 1880s, when it faded in face of the cheap competition from manuscript copies. The earliest certain date on any of these printed texts is in fact that on the volume from which 'The Stork Decides a Case' was taken, December 1848. Though many of them are undated, the indications are that the greatest activity was in the 1850s, which happens to tie in with the legend that Kim Chŏngho, the famous map-maker, financed his serious work by publishing popular novels. However, we must be cautious in thinking about the number of copies which were printed. The fact that so few have survived indicates that the number may never have been large, and the fact that blocks of 1848 could still be used to produce perfect copies in 1890 would seem to indicate that they had not suffered heavy wear.

We must also ask where the publisher got his stories from to publish. In two or three cases it seems clear from the print that a fairly nice manuscript was used for the engraving of the blocks, but in most cases the text has clearly been written specifically in order to make the blocks. The sources then could be almost anything. The publisher could simply have recollected a story he had heard told, and written it down in his own words. He could have made his own version in Korean of a story which he had written in Chinese. Only the most painstaking detailed research on the works will enable us to tell, and even then we may not succeed.

For the main problem still to be resolved is the relationship between the orally transmitted stories and the written, or printed, stories. 'Oral literature' is a concept which seems to be very useful in the study of societies which have no system of writing at all, and, in the absence in the past of any clear dating for any novels from pre-modern Korea, there has been a distinct tendency to give greater antiquity to oral traditions in Korea. However, there are dangers in thinking in that way about a society like that in Korea in the 19th century, which had had a system of writing of its own for four centuries and a respect for the written word which went back more than a thousand years. It would be perfectly possible in such a society for a written story from long ago to be picked up by a story teller and retold in his own way, giving rise to an oral tradition which might seem to go back to the beginning of time if one could not identify its origin.

In Korea we have evidence of a particular style of story telling to musical accompaniment, called in Korean *p'ansori*, from the second half of the 18th century onwards. The performance of *p'ansori* became hereditary, and a high degree of literary achievement was attained in this oral art. We also know, in fact, that it was not achieved purely through oral processes, since we have the actual works of a well educated man, Sin Chaehyo, who rewrote all the stories in the repertoire of the *p'ansori* artists in the 1870s and 1880s. Unfortunately these are the earliest recorded versions of any of the actual texts of these stories as told in *p'ansori* and this is already twenty to thirty years later than the heyday, if the term may be used, of the printed novel.

If therefore, we have both a printed novel and a telling of *p'ansori* provenance of the same story, we have problems in deciding which might have preceded the other. It was by no means difficult for mid-19th century writers to write in late 18th century style, since little had changed apart from some minor conventions of spelling, and these printed versions of novels tend to be rather plain in expression, as if they had been scribbled in rather a hurry. On the other hand, the oral versions tend to be adorned with rather fine-sounding literary phrases, but this means very little. The *p'ansori* performer could have picked up only the day before his performance any number of mellifluous and impressively antique phrases from Chinese — rather as the stork did in settling his case.

The two most popular purely Korean stories are both such a case. 'The Story of Ch'unhyang' is probably the better known outside Korea, and, being a story of young lovers crossed by the harsh rules of society, appealed greatly to mid 20th century Koreans. A version derived from the oral tradition is the third story in 'Virtuous Women'. The printed version has as yet only been translated into Russian, from Aston's copy in Leningrad. The second is 'The Story of Sim Ch'ŏng', a story of filial piety, which may not have had the appeal of the story of young lovers for a brief period recently, but one which reaches right down to the deepest level of moral values in the orient, and which now seems to have regained the lead in popularity which it has usually held over 'Ch'unhyang'.

Both these stories have appeared in hundreds of versions and been told through all media; books, children's comics, films, radio and television, but we are concerned primarily with the two versions which existed by the end of the 19th century in print. Both stories were printed in Chŏnju in versions derived from *p'ansori* performances, and earlier in straighter, written versions printed in Seoul,

The Chŏnju version of 'The Story of Sim Ch'ŏng' has been excellently translated into English by Marshall R. Phil, and we hope that his translation will be published before we are in print. To illustrate the very different natures which two such versions of what is, by title, the same story can have, we present here next our translation of the printed novel. It is certain that this existed before the Chŏnju version was published, and we have argued elsewhere that this Seoul version is probably very much older, perhaps as early as 1880.

The Story of Sim Ch'ŏng

Translated From a Book

Such as Young Ladies Read

One Hundred and Fifty Years Ago

It is related that, in the time when the Ch'eng-hua Emperor reigned in Ming, there lived in the Southern Counties a well known gentleman of the Sim clan whose name was Hyŏn. His branch of the clan was proud and great, and he was of the rank of Duke, but he cared nothing for honours and was one of the great scholars of his age.

His wife was of one of the best families, of the Chŏng clan, a true lady of most delicate features. She had resided with the Duke for more than ten years and given not the slightest cause for dissatisfaction. The only thing was that there was no offspring of the marriage, and therefore husband and wife communed in continuing sadness.

Then the lady had a God-given dream, and, as a result, she conceived in that month, and in the tenth month gave birth to a daughter. They were grieved that it was not a son, but they saw that she was an extraordinarily attractive girl and they loved her. They gave her the personal name of Ch'ŏng, which means 'Purity', and the second name of Mongsŏn, which means 'Dream Fairy'. She was to them 'a precious jewel in the palm of the hand'.

Time passed and Ch'ŏng grew. In her third year she had not only beauty of looks and prodigious talents, but she was also gifted with such extreme devotion to her parents that the neighbours and relatives all praised and admired her.

But 'in the fullness of joy comes grief' has always been the way of the world, and the Lady Chŏng was suddenly taken by an illness which proved fatal. She departed this world, and the

Duke mourned her greatly. He buried her with all due ceremonies and held his daughter Ch'ŏng to himself in sadness day and night. Ch'ŏng too called upon and wailed for her mother. One could not have borne to look upon the misery of father and daughter.

The Duke's household gradually went into decline, and he became so ridden with illness that he could not leave his bed. Worse, he developed eye trouble, and before many months could not discern things a few inches away. His life was ever more shabby. He sold off all his few family possessions to keep them in food from day to day, and then was desperate.

As time passed and Ch'ŏng grew up, she was so saddened by the deprivations which her father suffered that she begged for food to provide for him from day to day around the neighbourhood. All were moved to pity for their misery and did not grudge to give.

One day Ch'ŏng went out and late in the day had not come home. The Duke was hungry and sunk deep in anxiety. He took up his walking stick, shuffled out in his straw sandals, and waited for her for a while, leaning on the gate Then he slowly made his way out to the road. Suddenly he missed his footing and fell into a pit. Try as he might, he could not move. His plight was truly critical, when an old priest, who happened to be passing, saw him, took hold of him and got him sitting up.

'Where,' he asked, 'were you going, incapacitated as you are, to get into this plight?'

'I am a blind man, as you can see,' the Duke sighed, 'and my child had gone out and not come home. I came out and was stumbling along aimlessly by myself. I was as good as dead when I was rescued by you. My indebtedness to you for your help is greater than the highest mountain'.

The old priest told him that he was a collector for the building of a Hall of the Law at the Heart in the Clouds Retreat in the Bright Moon Mountains. 'I came down to the village and was begging for alms when I happened to be passing ths spot and rescued you, sir. I see in your face that, though now you are destitute, in four or five years you will be one of the highest in the land and your daughter's glory will be the greatest in the whole world. But if you will make just one large donation, not only will your daughter be ennobled, but your blind eyes, sir, will be opened.'

'How much should I donate?'

'As a donation for the building of a Hall of the Law, a rice offering to the Buddha is the most important. You must donate three hundred bushels of polished rice.'

'Write "three hundred bushels of polished rice" in your donors' book,' said the Duke, and turned for home.

The old priest gestured his thanks to him with his hands together as in prayer. 'I will come again in a few days,' he said, and went on his way.

When the Duke got home, he sighed. 'I am a blind man who cannot even supply myself with thin rice and water. My young child ekes out my life with her begging. How can I get three hundred bushels to donate? If one breaks a promise to the Buddha, ill must come of it. Since I seem bound to break my promise, I cannot escape the billion hells in the next life.'

He was still thinking these unhappy thoughts when Ch'ŏng brought home the food she had begged. Seeing her father's unhappiness, she was disturbed.

'Today I went over to the rich house on the west side and ground their mortar for them. By the time I could get home with the food I got, of course it was very late. This unhappiness of yours, dear father, is all due to the shallowness of my care for you.'

The Duke dried his tears. 'I've been brooding lately. The hardness of our lot is "a vexation which cuts me to the marrow". I went out of doors. I was groping my way along, with nowhere particular to go, and careless of where I put my feet, when I fell into a pit. I would have died, but I was found by a begging priest' — he gave her the details — 'who told me that both my blindness and our having to beg for a living was a punishment for sins in a previous life, and if I donated three hundred bushels of polished rice, my eyes would be opened and you would have great honour for the rest of your life. This gave me a sudden desire to redeem myself, and I told him to write down three hundred bushels in his donors' book. When I came home and thought about it, you and I have no way of earning a farthing in cash or a pint of rice, so where can we turn to make such a donation? I am going to have to break a promise to the Buddha and in future will suffer great damnation. That is why I am unhappy.'

Having heard him, Ch'ŏng tried to console him. 'Don't be unhappy, father. They say that if one is utterly sincere, heaven is moved. It was because you are as sincere as you are that you wanted to make a donation, so there will be help from the Buddha. Please don't worry yourself unncessarily.'

She prepared his supper at once and served it to him, but the Duke did not eat. He only sighed long, and his eyes were filled with a stream of tears. Ch'ŏng felt great pity for him and consoled him with gentle words. 'Heaven is high, but sees clearly. Heaven and Earth, Sun and Moon will be moved by your sincerity, father. Do not be excessively distressed.'

She consoled him in every way she could think of, but in truth she could see no way out. She went over every possible plan, and then at midnight that night she bathed and purified herself, went down into the garden, spread a mat and prayed to Heaven.

'The human being, Sim Ch'ŏng, would not shirk death for her blind father's sake. My father, praying that his closed eyes be opened, now wishes to make a donation to the Buddha, but he has no way of getting three hundred bushels of polished rice. So, instead, he has come to commit the sin of breaking a promise to the Buddha. O Gods of Heaven and Earth, look upon him.'

All through the night she prayed and when she went back into her room, could not get to sleep. She sighed with grief until she drowsed off. The old priest appeared before her.

'Tomorrow,' he said, 'there will be someone wishing to buy you. Though you will be sold to go to a place where you will die, do not shirk it. Heaven is moved by your devotion to your father, and it is certain that in the place of death you will find honour.'

Suddenly he was gone, and she awoke to find that it had been but 'a dream beneath the shade of a tree'. Greatly puzzled in her heart, she waited for the dawn, contemplating their situation.

Now there was a merchant of the Southern Capital who journeyed to and fro from the Northern Capital with his cargoes and travelled all countries trading. Year by year as he crossed the Great Sea, he passed a water called 'The Phosphorescent Pool' in the region of the Glass Kingdom. In this water there was a demon. Unimportant boats could go their way unharmed, but any ships heavily laden with treasures and silks could only pass in safety after a human sacrifice had been made to the Water God. Therefore, year by year, he would buy a girl child to put into the Phosphorescent Pool as he went by it.

At this time there was a man once more going round all the villages calling. When Ch'ŏng heard him, she was so happy that she rushed out and asked whether he would consider buying a child like her. The man looked at her and saw no ordinary girl. Devotion to her parents shone in her eyes, her eyebrows were like sketches of hills in the spring, her lips seemed to be painted with cinnabar, her high ears shone with the light of the sun and the moon, her shoulders were like a swallow's wings and her slender waist as as if bound with silk gauze. She was 'in every way most fair to look upon', the rarest beauty in the world, and with the signs of a perfect fortune. Yet her clothes were tatters which barely covered her flesh, she was nothing but skin and bone, and through her dishevelled hair the worry on her face showed clearly. It was as if 'the indigo flowers in the cinnamon palace' had been hit by a wild wind. Her jangling voice was like that of a young phoenix screeching from high in the sky. How could that merchant, born and brought up in the uncultured outlands, and always busy in uncivilised parts, have seen such a noble girl of matchless beauty?

With a flurried bow he said, 'I beg your pardon. I'm just a merchant who buys and sells goods. I buy a girl for a good price and sacrifice her to the Dragon Spirit as I go by the Phosphorescent Pool. Murdering human beings, I am amassing sins, but, on the other hand, this is my life. I heard you calling now, young lady, and came to you. I cannot see in your face that you look as if you are destined to drown. What can have brought you to want to be sold?'

Ch'ŏng burst into tears. 'My stars have led me along a rugged way. I could tell you all the details of my life, but the longer it went on the more fate cast me down. My father is blind, and my heart was breaking with my consciousness of my obligations to him. Then on' — she gave the date — 'an old priest, passing by, saw my father and told me that I should not shirk fire or water to do my duty to my father. Though I sell myself and come to the place of death, if my father again sees the sun and moon, I may go to the Ninth Plain, but mine will be a happy ghost. I hope that you will give three hundred bushels of polished rice to purchase me.'

When she had finished, the merchant was moved by the pitifulness of her plight and her extreme devotion to her father. 'I am in two minds whether to buy you or not, young lady, but you are extremely devoted to your father, and man is not wood or stone. How can I not be impressed? If it were my decision alone, I would just give three hundred bushels of rice and go on my way without ay regrets. However, this is a business which concerns several partners, and it is proper that I should go back to them and discuss the delivery of the rice.'

Ch'ŏng accepted this, and went in. For the moment she deceived her father. 'Some rich man of the village on the other side who has no children has always loved me and been generous in giving me food for you. Now I have sold myself to that rich man for three hundred bushels of polished rice so that you can make your donation. When did the begging priest say that he would come?'

When the Duke heard this, he was on the one hand happy, but, on the other, when he thought of his daughter going to somebody else's house, his heart was broken. He shed tears as he said, 'According to what you say, I can avoid breaking a promise to the Buddha, and am really happy about that, but if you have been sold to another for a good price, you cannot stay in my house a moment longer. Who do you think I can look to to keep me alive, all alone?'

He wept sadly, and Ch'ŏng, who had still not told her father the truth, felt as if she were coming apart inside. 'If he is so unhappy,' she thought, 'at my being alive but going where I shall be well clothed and well fed, if I were to tell him that I am going to the place where I will die, certainly he would not live on in this world. Can there be anyone as unfilial as I among either the living or the dead?' The tears she wept swelled the rivers.

Before long the merchant delivered the rice, just as the begging priest came to the door asking to see them. Ch'ŏng gave him the rice she had got from the merchant, and the priest thanked her endlessly.

After he had had the rice taken away and gone, Ch'ŏng asked the merchant what day he was going to take her.

'We are setting sail,' the merchant said, 'on the third day of the seventh month this autumn,' and he left.

Ch'ŏng sat down quietly and thought that it was only a matter of three days or so to the day she should die. She could only pray to Heaven.

'Now my father cannot see what is in front of him, and, though he has me, if I go out and do not come home for half a day, there is no one to ladle him out a spoonful of water, and he waits for me. When I die, who will look after my father and bring him to his old age? He will certainly not be able to avoid starving to death before many days. What will happen to me in future for having caused him such sorrow? Alas! In the thirteen years since I became acquainted with this world I have not known my dear mother's face. When I served my ailing father, I was not able to get enough food to fill him, and could not provide him with clothes for the cold and the heat. My clothes have never had neck bands, and my skirts have never been full. Instead I forgot such things, and, seeing my father at his last gasp, I wept bitterly day and night as I went to the east to beg food and to the west to seek sustenance for him, never giving a backward glance at propriety or shame. Now I am abandoning my father and even going to the place of death. My troubled soul will slip off to the clouded sky and I will embrace my mother with tears. It cannot be avoided.'

Such thoughts made her feel that her heart was breaking and her insides melting away. From that day on she begged diligently and collected food, which she cooked and served frequently to her father.

In no time at all the day fixed by the merchant arrived. Ch'ŏng realised that she could not deceive her father in the end, and thereupon threw herself on her face at her father's knees wailing sadly. The Duke was taken by surprise, and urgently enquired the reason for this, but Ch'ŏng's heart was so full of sadness that she could not put it into words. The Duke also wailed and caressed his daughter as he asked the reason for her sadness.

Ch'ŏng managed to pull herself together. 'That three hundred bushels of rice the other day,' she said, 'was not from a local rich man. To cut a long story short, I got it by selling myself to a merchant, and now he has come to take me. I didn't tell you this from the start, because I was worried that I would cause you to be angry with me, father, while I was still with you. Today it is time for farewells, for our last parting, so I am telling you my true feelings. Alas, our love for each other, father and daughter, is ten times greater than anyone else's. The way you reared me, who had no mother, and the way, when I was barely acquainted with the world, you went blind, your family line came to an end, and we were not able to get enough to eat, no one has had a life like ours. Now it is worse. When I ponder how I am abandoning you, to become a resentful spirit in the water, my regret at having failed you is immeasurable.'

She wept distractedly, and the Duke, having heard what she said, immediately wailed in a loud voice. 'My child, what words are these? Even if I had broken my promise to the Buddha, and gone to the million, million hells, not to return for ten million years, how could you have been so bold as to scheme to kill me with indecent haste? Even with you here I have sadness in plenty. Alone, on whom am I to rely for my life, tell me? I would rather just follow you to death.'

He beat his body as he wailed out loud.

The people of the village, seeing the sudden swooning lamentation of Ch'ŏng and her father, and enquiring of the cause of it, each felt pity for them. 'How Tzu-lü carried food to feed his parents, and how Meng-tsung's tears produced bamboo shoots to please his mother are famous stories from long ago, but we have never heard tell of anyone being born with such great love for their father that they would sell their body to a place of death to realise their father's wish. No man of old can match the resolute devotion to her father of this thirteen year old girl. Poor child! From the age of seven or eight Sim Ch'ŏng's miserable hardship grew worse and worse. We have always bemoaned the fact that riches and honours and poverty and lowliness are unjustly apportioned, but what can be the sense of her not being able to avoid becoming a resentful spirit in the water?'

Many were those who were sad for Ch'ŏng's sake.

Ch'ŏng dried her tears, and, facing all her neighbours from either side, bowed to them and begged them sadly, 'Ladies and gentlemen, if you will extend the charity of your hearts to my ailing father, save him, and protect him through his remaining years, though I go to the Ninth Plain, I will repay your kindness with bunches of grass from the Mountain of Flowers and mouthfuls of pearls from the Lake of Longevity.'

Several people were so deeply concerned for Sim Ch'ŏng that they grasped her and consoled her, saying, 'Even if you had not said so, we are so used to admiring your devotion to your father that we would have done the right thing. We will think of you and take special care of your father, don't worry. Since you are already on your way to your place of death, it is proper that you should die, and perhaps in a later life repay what we do for you in this world by becoming the child of one of our families.'

Others said, 'Heaven is supremely fair, yet is it making her, at the tender age of thirteen, into a resentful spirit in the water? It must surely be testing her.'

Ch'ŏng, begging sadly for her life, entreated the merchant to let her have just one more day so that all bitterness might be removed from the unspent love between her father and her before they went. The merchant for his part was so impressed by her inborn devotion to her father, and felt so sorry for their situation, that he went away telling her to stay a few days more. Duke Sim, exhausted with lamentation, just cried without ceasing that he wanted to go with her.

Soon the few days passed and the merchant came again. He gave them fifty bushels more of polished rice, saying, 'We have been so moved by the young lady's enormous devotion to her father that we are giving fifty bushels more so that the young lady's father may have sustenance for three or four years.' At the same time he asked her to go. Ch'ŏng thanked him a hundred times and took the rice, which she entrusted to a respectable family in the village with earnest entreaties.

She entered the shrine to her mother to make her farewells. Her bitter lamentation pierced the Ninth Heaven. If the spirit of the Lady Chŏng recognized her voice, how could she not be moved?

With the greatest reluctance, Ch'ŏng took leave of her father. Father and daughter, face touching face, exhausted themselves with lamentation, until presently Ch'ŏng pulled herself together, and, stroking her father's hand, said, 'Father, I am unworthy of you. You must believe that I never existed if you are to relieve yourself of any burden on your conscience. I have managed to provide for you still, and pray that you will continue to live long hereafter. I shall not see you again in this life, but wish that, since it is right that we should become father and daughter in a later life, we will fulfil all that we have felt for each other in this life.'

Having expressed her undying love, she pulled herself up. The Duke grasped his daughter, and, stamping his feet, lamented, 'Who do you mean me to depend on? Where do you mean me to go?'

After consoling him in every way she could think of, Ch'ŏng had to say farewell. Then, as she went out through the door, she felt so faint that she could not help stumbling at every step. If even one with a heart of wood or stone had seen how she looked then, they could not have repressed feelings of sadness.

The Duke groped his way outside with difficulty, beating his breast and stamping his feet, lamenting, 'Ch'ŏng, Ch'ŏng, where are you going, daring to abandon me?' His misery knew no bounds. But the situation had to be accepted, there was nothing to be done, Ch'ŏng knew, as she went out, carrying her immense burden of grief and looking back at her father. She stumbled ten times at every step.

At every house people came to their doors and gazed at Ch'ŏng going on her way. They sighed long and said to each other, 'What devotion to her father she has! We are seeing today such a thing as has never been seen in all the ages.'

Ch'ŏng was scarcely able to make her way. She reached the Phosphorescent Pool, where all the merchants were waiting impatiently with their goods displayed, feeling uneasy that it was getting too late. When they saw Ch'ŏng coming, they told her to get aboard quickly. Ch'ŏng felt that she had failed her father, but there was nothing she could do about it. Looking up to Heaven, she lamented, and then again, facing in each direction, bowed and said:

'Ch'ŏng, daughter of the ailing human Sim Hyŏn, lost her mother at the age of three. She kept her father, who could not see in front of him, alive by begging for food with which to feed him. Then, when told that if a donation were given to the Buddha, his eyes would be opened, she sold herself to be cast into the water to die. Dying itself is nothing to be sad about, but from today there is no one to serve my ailing father even one spoonful of water. Certainly he will think of his dying daughter and die from his illness. I have no way to gather up his corpse after his death and give him permanent burial amongst his ancestors' graves. I was the child of a man, and have parted from him, he alive and I to die, without having repaid my parents for having given me birth and upbringing. I am dying before my father. I am casting my body, given to me by my parents, into the billows of the boundless sea to be food for the fish. In heaven or on earth can there be such lack of love for one's parents as this? Eternal blue Heaven, shining spirits of Heaven and Earth, look upon me!'

After she had finished praying, she bent over to look at the water. The blue waters stretched to the sky. A sad breeze rose gently. A cloud grew and wrapped her in its vastness. A song from the sailors urged her soul on its way. How sad and pitiable!

Ch'ŏng called upon her father three times in lamentation, covered her face with both hands and leapt flying into the water. All the merchants, seeing her miserable plight, grieved deeply.

Now when this happened, Ch'ŏng did not sink as she fell into the water, but floated away for a while. Suddenly a perfumed breeze arose, and floating on it came fairies in a small boat, with their hair done up in the style for a funeral ceremony, playing jade flutes and seeming to fly. They took hold of Ch'ŏng, lifted her into the boat, took off her soaked clothes and changed them for a set of new clothes. They poured some life-reviving potion from a jade jar and gave it her to drink.

Shortly Ch'ŏng opened her eyes and saw her own body lying in comfort. Fairies such as she had never seen before, dressed in clothes of many colours, were sitting on either side of her, massaging her hands and feet. Ch'ŏng was very happy, but astonished, and, sitting up quickly, she raised her hands in thanks.

'All you fairy ladies — who are you that you rescue people who have died by falling in the water?' At least, such were her words, but she was so faint in spirit that she could get no sound out.

'We are ladies-in-waiting of the Dragon King of the Eastern Sea,' replied the fairies. 'He told us to escort you to him, madam. We were so late that you were already near to "suffering the fate of a crushed jewel or a fallen flower".'

Ch'ŏng was recovering consciousness. 'I am a human being of humble origin,' she said. 'I am extremely grateful that the Dragon King should have such care for me.'

'Your penance, lady,' the fairies said, 'was determined by Heaven, and the Dragon King's summoning you now is also Heaven's decree. When you go to him, you will understand all.'

As they rowed the boat, they sang a fairy song to the playing of jade flutes. Ch'ŏng felt as fresh in heart as if her body were flying. In the twinkling of an eye they reached the place. A palace of pearls with halls of mother-of-pearl shimmered in a mist. On the main gate was a sign on a board engraved in letters of gold: DRAGON PALACE OF THE EASTERN SEA. The fairies brought the boat to the steps before the gate and requested her to land. Ch'ŏng raised herself and alighted. From within there came out in pairs ladies-in-waiting dressed in red embroidered court robes. They brought out a palanquin of gold and said, 'Young lady, please take this palanquin.'

Ch'ŏng demurred. 'I am a human being of low birth. How can I ride in this?'

'Lady,' the fairies said, 'in human life you were out of your time and lived in poverty and hardship, but in our watery regions you are an extremely honoured person, and in former days you used to ride in this very palanquin. Do not demur, but take your seat quickly. Remember that the Great King is waiting.'

Ch'ŏng protested three times, but then, unable to refuse, got in. All the ladies-in-waiting escorted her, performing for her all the music suitable to the occasion. Six dragons bore the palanquin. She was splendidly majestic, with all the airs of a fairy spirit.

They passed through many gates and reached the foot of the throne. The jade balustrade glistened, the pearl curtain was dazzling. The whole place was lost in shrouds of mist and clouds of awesome majesty. Her spirit was all the more ill at ease and her thoughts confused. A pair of ladies-in-waiting took hold of the young lady and led her up to the throne. Pointing to the throne on the north side, they told her to present herself. When the young lady looked up, she saw the King on the golden throne. On his head he had the ruler's crown. He was wearing formal robes of green silk, with a belt at his waist of lustrous white pearls, and clasping a sceptre of jasper. He was seated haughtily, impressively glorious. On either side courtiers held phoenix-tail fans. It was a majestic and awesome scene.

When Ch'ŏng stepped forward and humbly made her obeisances before him, the Dragon King bowed. 'Ah, K'uei,' he said (K'uei being the Chinese name for the constellation Andromeda), 'and how did you enjoy being a human being?'

Ch'ŏng made another humble obeisance and said, 'This unworthy female is a human being of low birth. I cannot understand Your Majesty's intent.'

The Dragon King smiled. 'In a previous existence you were the noble lady of King Chien of Ch'u. You were given charge of the wine at the Queen Mother's banquet at the Gemstone Lake, but, being partial to Lord Lao, you gave him much wine to drink, and there was not enough wine for the feast. The Lord of the Heaven where Lord Lao resided demanded of the Jade Emperor that punishment be given. The Jade Emperor, wrathful, said, "This is not the crime of heavenly beings, but the crime of a serving woman in charge of wine. Let a close investigation be made and severe punishment be given."

'Lord Lao was to be banished to the human world and live forty years without any harm coming to him, he said, and then you were to become his daughter and show your devotion to him. So, forty years after Lord Lao become Sim Hyŏn and descended to the human world, you became his daughter. For the crime of having misappropriated wine in heaven, you were given no angel to feed you, and were made to beg for your food for thirteen years. For him, his eyes were to be dimmed, and he was to be fed with what you, K'uei, begged for him. So it was determined that you would pay for what you had done in heaven. Getting one's deserts for a former life and suffering and pleasure in the present life are all fates as determined by Heaven.

'However, the Jade Emperor had still not dissipated all his anger. When he held court, with all the immortals of the world, the Dragon Kings of the Four Seas, the Mountain Gods of the Five Hills, all the Buddhas and all the Rulers of Heavens assembled, Sakyamuni made a submission to the Jade Emperor:

'"It is already eight or nine years since Lord Lao, in the midst of the increasingly severe suffering he was experiencing in the human world, became unable to make out things a few inches away. He will have paid fully for his sins. Although K'uei's sin of having disobeyed Heaven's command is not slight, she descended to the human world, had hardship and difficulty from babyhood, and begged east and west for food to serve to Lord Lao. Heaven and earth were filled with her devotion to her father. It was enough to pay for her sins in her previous life, but she did more. She sold her body to go to its death. Her dedication to her father's well-being is indeed miraculous. Therefore your servant sent his disciple to test her heart, and found the behaviour of father and daughter to be in fact utterly sincere. Only to punish the sins of a former life and not to take gracious account of honest devotion to one's parents in the present life is not a just dispensation of the Court of Heaven, and their dedication moves one to pity. Your Majesty, send down the rain and dew of your graciousness and make clear judgment between the good and the not good."

'The Jade Emperor was persuaded by these words, and at once ordered Nan-tou (that is to say, Sirius) to bestow blessings and income, and Pei-tou (Charles' Wain) to bestow a name and descendants.

'Nan-tou reported:

'"K'uei was originally the noble daughter of the Dragon King of the Eastern Sea, and, descending to the human world, was of a pious and honourable nature. It is impossible that she should become the mother of a commoner family. It is in order that she should become the Queen of the Glass Kingdom, and I am arranging that she should have a full life of royal pleasure."

'The Jade Emperor consented.

'Pei-tou in turn reported:

'"Since Nan-tou has made all possible arrangements for K'uei, your servant is arranging that Lord Lao should become a Grand Duke, meet a falling star late in life, have sons and daughters, and be the richest, most honoured and best provided for in his generation, and that then, at the age of seventy five, he should return to his former office, while K'uei should have three sons and two daughters and, at the age of seventy three, return again to the Eastern Sea."

'The Jade Emperor gave his gracious consent, and I made a request of him in my turn. "You are good enough to forgive K'uei's sins. Your servant shared with her the love between father and daughter also in a previous life. In a few days' time, K'uei is to end her life at the Phosphorescent Pool, and I cannot but rescue her from that dire strait. Let me rescue her, as is proper, keep her for one night, and send her to the human world."

'The Jade Emperor consented, so you were brought here to stay the night, so that we might resume the enjoyment of the love of father and daughter. Tomorrow you return.'

When Ch'ŏng heard this, she realised that all that had happened from first to last was predestined. More unhappy than ever, she prostrated herself upon the ground and said, 'When I hear Your Majesty's explanation, I know that my sinfulness in a previous life was manifest, so I do not complain. However, when I think of the penance which is past, my ailing father's present deprivation and his likely dying of sorrow, I am as if torn apart inside.'

'Now,' said the Dragon King, 'your penance is all done, and in future you will enjoy everlasting blessings and prosperity. Do not be sad.'

He ordered the ladies-in-waiting to bring tea and fruit for her to have. Presently the ladies-in-waiting brought tea on a purple platter. The tea was like mist over the pearly ball of a full moon and the fruit like jujubes. As Ch'ŏng took them, her spirits stirred, and the recalled clearly all her former life.

She was happy again to see the royal face of her father, the King. The ladies-in-waiting on each side of her, who were all the same as had attended her very self in her former life, could not restrain their pleasure either. It was as yesterday that, being in charge of the vintage wine, she had felt sorry for Lord Lao and stolen the wine to give him, and again she could not repress her sadness. Looking up at her father, she wept.

'When I think of how I suffered penance in the human world, I am shocked. Now that I have entered this place, I wish not to leave it again, but to stay here.'

'Don't be sad,' her father said. 'If you leave again for the human world, your penance of former days will be "a spring dream of another place". How could you disobey the command of Heaven?'

He ordered the ladies-in-waiting to conduct Ch'ŏng to a separate hall in the rear gardens, and to see that she rested comfortably. Ch'ŏng followed the ladies-in-waiting, and, when she got to the hall, all the things displayed in the hall were those she had seen in former days.

Meanwhile Sim Hyŏn, hovering between life and death, wanted at least to see his daughter going out of the gate to wherever it was she was going, but, since his eyes were closed, how could he see her? He just beat his breast in lamentation until suddenly he fainted and could not regain consciousness. The people of the neighbourhood, feeling sorry for him in his plight, took hold of him and saved his life by rubbing his hands and feet and pouring hot water on them. Presently Sim Hyŏn came to his senses, and beat the wall with his hand in lamentation.

'My poor daughter! At three you lost your mother. When, a helpless baby in a quilt, you cried for your mother, what could I, an invalid, feel? I was clinging to life, not quite dead, and on top of that I became blind and could not make out things a foot away. Our family fortune was exhausted and we could not get food for a single meal a day. My daughter, you begged in cold and heat alike to ensure that I was not hungry even for a moment. Now look what has become of you for your father's sake: your dedication is extreme, but how can I hope to live? Had great broad Heaven had mercy on me, I might have been destitute but my eyes healthy, or I might not have been able to see with my eyes but have had wealth and to spare, then how could you have gone to all that trouble to go to a place where you would die? Alas! Even a child dying of an illness is pitiful. I, a chronic invalid, have sent my devoted daughter to an immediate, untimely and tragic death. Even if the Spirits of Heaven and Earth were not to think it wrong to open my eyes, how could I, living alone, endure and beat this sadness?'

In this way day and night he called on Ch'ŏng in lamentation. The people of the neighbourhood were unable to bear the sound of his weeping, and could not sleep for it. Hyŏn, night and day alike, lamented bitterly alone. To console himself he groped and found the food which Ch'ŏng had begged to collect for him. He groped all around and found that every bowl was filled with dishes of dried meat and cooked food. As he handled each one, his chest tightened and his stomach turned to jelly. Try as he might to control his sorrow, he could not. He called upon his daughter once again.

'My poor child! You fed your ailing father and kept him alive like this, yet I coolly send you to your place of death. How can one call that humanity?'

So he passed the months in lamentation day and night until autumn was all over and winter was upon him. The snow-bearing wind whined and cut into the bones of men. In the desolate, deserted house there was little sign of human life, and all he thought of was Ch'ŏng. He became an emaciated skeleton.

Now the family to which the fifty bushels of polished rice had been entrusted was well off, and only an aged couple in it. Furthermore, they were honest by nature and respected for their virtue. So, even when Ch'ŏng was alive, they had not grudged to give them generous gifts of food. Ch'ŏng had been deeply grateful. After she had gone, entrusting the rice to them, they were even more sympathetic. They served every meal to Sim devotedly and fed him religiously. They chopped wood to heat his room, and looked after him carefully.

When Hyŏn thought of the life-long hardship which faced him, an invalid, completely indebted to others, he wanted to die, but it was Heaven's decree, and he was not allowed to achieve his wish. Thus the first autumn month of the next year was upon him, and the anniversary of the day Ch'ŏng had gone to die arrived in due course. The autumn wind was doleful, and the calls of the geese seeking their flocks as they went south pierced the heart. The voices of the crickets in the kitchen sounded like a rushing stream, and disturbed the dreams into which Hyŏn had fallen with difficulty. He wept sadly, calling upon his daughter, less able than ever to get properly to sleep.

To continue the story of Sim Ch'ŏng, she had passed one night in the Dragon Palace, and when she got up she had completely forgotten the events of her previous life. She was eager only to get out and see her father again as soon as she could. She was completely at a loss as to what to do, when a lady-in-waiting entered, ordered by the Dragon King to summon her. Ch'ŏng quickly obeyed, and the Dragon King said, 'We were given leave by the Jade Emperor to spend one night together making each other happy. That was a delightful surprise, but, though it is sad that you are departing again, it is not something that we can refuse to do. So, back you go to the world of men.'

He ordered the attendants to send her off in a palanquin. The ladies-in-waiting obeyed and went out, with Ch'ŏng in the palanquin, to the shore of the sea. There they put her into a small boat and rowed her along to the appointed place.

'Here,' said the fairies in farewell, 'is the place where, before, you threw yourself into the water, madam. Here is where we leave you.'

In a flash they were gone, and the lotus leaf boat changed into a flower bud quite big enough inside to take her body. The flower was most strange, with layer upon layer of petals. The young lady could only look to the east and give a gesture of thanks.

When she was thirsty, she drank the dew which gathered in the petals of the flower, and was sated and content. It was the ambrosia, one draft of which would automatically cure all human ills: what a miraculous treasure!

Meanwhile the merchants who had bought the young lady to set her in the water, were on their way back, having traded their goods. When they reached the Phosphorescent Pool, they sighed and lamented all over again. 'Last year we left in this water a girl of the Sim family' (and the reader should of course know that the name Sim is written with the character which means 'to sink into water') 'whom we had bought, with high hopes, and now our company has returned safely. It is sad and pitiful to think how that girl prayed.'

They were going along, talking with each other, and making music, when suddenly they saw a multi-coloured cloud form on the surface of the water, and out of nowhere a flower bud as big as a large dining table floating about on the water. They had never before seen such glorious colours. All the merchants marvelled. 'We have been travelling for years and never seen a leaf of a tree, never mind a flower. This flower is so unusual that it must be that the girl's spirit has turned into a flower, and she has not left the place where she died. The proper thing to do is to take it and present it to the King.'

They fished out the flower and put it in a jade bowl. When they presented it to the King of the country, he was overjoyed with the flower. After rewarding the merchants handsomely, he called for a first class workman to make up a multi-coloured cabinet. The flower was put into the cabinet and left near his bed-chamber. After the court had been dismissed in the morning, he would sit in front of the cabinet, enamoured. The fragrance was overpowering, and, since a multi-coloured cloud formed, he could not see exactly what was inside it. Its beauty grew more glorious day by day, and it seemed to be continuously smiling at the King, so that he never left it for a moment.

Meanwhile Sim Ch'ŏng hid herself inside the flower, maintaining herself on ambrosia. Occasionally, when no one was there, she came out of the cabinet and took a look all around, but when she saw any sign of anyone, she hid inside the flower, so that no one could know about her. At that time the King was not getting on well with the Queen, and, as soon as the court was dismissed in the morning, he would go to the flower cabinet. His love for it grew morning and evening.

In her unhappiness the Queen took ill. All known medicines were ineffective, and eventually she passed to her rest. She was buried with due ceremony at Sŏnnŭng. After the period of court mourning was over, the courtiers addressed the King. 'The Inner Hall of the Kingdom cannot be left empty even for a short time. We humbly beseech Your Majesty to select a lady of a family of learning and virtue for your consort, and not to disappoint the people in their hopes.'

The King heard their submission, and said, 'I cannot be without a queen even for a short while, but, however wise a lady is found, should she not be congenial, the whole country will be disappointed. Therefore I hesitate. Stay withdrawn still, my lords.'

The courtiers left the court and the king went out as usual to the lotus flower cabinet. Suddenly the air was filled with fragrance, and he saw a girl as beautiful as a fairy child disappear rapidly into the cabinet. The King was astonished, and quickly went forward and opened the door of the cabinet. On previous days a coloured cloud had dazzled him, but today the cloud cleared, the flower had disappeared, and all he saw was the most beautiful girl in the world, dressed in multi-coloured clothes and a red skirt. Her age was some thirteen or fourteen. Her lustrous skin and outstanding air made her truly 'a beauty worth the loss of a kingdom'.

The King was astonished and delighted. He examined her carefully two or three times and found that not only was she extraordinarily attractive, but virtue was apparent in her appearance and she had all the signs of being destined to prosper. She was 'a true consort of a king with a thousand chariots' and 'mother of a country with a people of ten thousand clans'. For a while he examined her carefully, bewitched and confused.

'Are you a fairy? Are you a spirit? How dare you hide inside a flower to make sport of a king?'

'I am neither a fairy,' replied the beauty humbly, with a modest expression on her face, 'nor a spirit. I am but a human girl, and to have allowed a flower made by fairies to hide me and come into this awesome place to dazzle Your Majesty's eyes, though not deliberate, is "a crime deserving ten thousand deaths".'

The King was even more puzzled by what she had said, and wanted to ask her for a precise explanation, but suddenly a boy eunuch announced: 'The Three Dukes and the Six Ministers request an extraordinary audience.'

The King guessed what the reason for this must be, and

immediately took the throne in the Hall of Love and Virtue. When he summoned the courtiers in, the Head of the Office of the Annals addressed him:

'When your servant was observing the sky last night, the star K'uei shone into the palace with imposing strength, and the vigour of the Tzu and Wei stars was rising. Certainly it is a sign that the girl who will become the Mother of the Country is lodged within the palace, and that when she succeeds to the throne of the Queen, a great prince will be born. Your servant offers his felicitations on the restoration of the Royal Household.'

The Minister Myŏng also addressed the King:

'Your servant has also been watching the sky recently. Since good omens surround Tou and Niu every night, Your Majesty should select from among the secondary wives one of talent and virtue and raise her to the rank of Queen, so as not to break faith with the expectations of the people.'

The King finally explained to them the facts of the matter that they had been talking about. When he told them of the looks, talents and virtue of the girl, the courtiers marvelled. They cheered and congratulated him, and advised him to choose an auspicious day of the year and hold the wedding soon. The King gave his gracious consent and had Royal Observatory select a day. It was barely a fortnight away.

'Since the Queen has no family, it is proper that she should be escorted to the Separate Palace for the marriage ceremony to be performed,' the King instructed. 'And let all the usual articles for the bride and groom be prepared.'

The courtiers obeyed the commands and withdrew. Officials made ready the wedding articles and awaited orders. When the auspicious day arrived, Miss Sim was escorted to the Separate Palace, supported by several thousand palace girls. When they had finished dressing her, make-up, accessories and all, at the appointed time the King performed the six ceremonies of marriage and went to the Separate Palace. He presented the pair of geese to Heaven and Earth, and handed the Queen into the phoenix palanquin, and a procession of carriages took her to her married home. They returned inside the palace, and in the Hall of Everlasting Fragrance they exchanged nuptial cups.

The King raised his head and saw that Queen Sim had on

her head a Double Phoenix Nine Flower Crown with twelve jewelled pendants which swung on her moon-like forehead. Her golden Phoenix Wing dress, with a sun and moon pattern, outshone the sun. On her slender hips a skirt of deep red Vietnamese silk seemed to hang like a many-coloured cloud. There was not a single precious thing that she did not have adorning her whole body, each vying with each other one as an omen of happiness. The bright, dazzling brilliance with which her attire shone made her extreme beauty, like that of the sun and the moon, even more ethereal. How could one of such virtue and such beauty of face be likened to something which had been seen inside a flower? The King was entranced, his love so extraordinary and his adoration so great as to make the highest mountain seem low and the rivers and seas seem shallow. How could one speak of this in the same breath as the bliss between any ordinary couple of any generation?

Such was his state that the King hated to leave her for a moment, and it had been several days since he had appeared in the Outer Halls. The officials of the court, civil and military, waited for the morning audience until it was so late that they just had to withdraw. The secondary wives of the Six Palaces and the three thousand palace girls waited to appear before the King, but retired disappointed.

The Queen felt very embarrassed, and one day counselled the King: 'Your Majesty's consort was, as you know, born into and brought up in a humble family, and knows nothing of the world. Much less can I speak on affairs of state. However, the grace of Heaven is infinite. Humble as I am, I have been thrust into this most noble position. Day and night I am filled with awe, respect and careful discretion. Therefore how can I regard Your Majesty's errors and not remonstrate with you? I have heard that, if the King neglects the affairs of state for one day, the people are in distress for a whole year, and that, if the people do not submit willingly, it is said to be because the King is without virtue. Since now Your Majesty has without due notice suspended the affairs of state for several days, what sort of a king will the court regard Your Majesty as in future? Since from of old, if the Ruler is beguiled by his lady, there is no one to protect the state, Your Majesty should take as his model the usage of the men of old, practise virtue, and not be held to account by future generations.'

The King came to his senses completely, and praised her, saying, 'Wise queen, remonstrating thus over my loss of virtue and bringing me to my senses. You rank with the Fairy Queen of King Hsüan of Chou and the Wise Wife of Duke Yang of Ch'i.'

Straightaway he came out to the Outer Halls and gave the courtiers their audience, and, after dismissing the court, entered the Inner Halls and gave the audience of the Six Palaces. Throughout the Inner and the Outer Halls of the palace the cheers rang, and they shook with the noise of the rejoicing. At noon the Golden Dragon Throne and the Coral Chair were set in the Court Hall. The King wore his Winged Cicada crown with jewelled pendants, his red silk Dragon Robe and his Pearl Belt, grasped his Jasper Sceptre, and in the royal eyes beamed an expression of complete joy. The Queen for her part wore on her head a Double Phoenix Nine Flower crown, on her body a silk jacket with design of kingfishers in crimson and gold, and a skirt embroidered in crimson and red. She sat composed upon her chair. A forest of ladies-in-waiting lined up in attendance to left and to right. A cloud of good omen enveloped the palace and a zephyr soothed men's hearts. Truly men were in harmony and the world was at peace. Then there was performed a full range of music: the pipes, flutes, drums and horns filled the air. Brocade mats glistened in the sun. This day's magnificent event can scarcely ever have been seen before.

Presently the court ladies bowed their heads, gathered up their red silk skirts, and made their farewell bows from the verandah. All members of the Royal Family, in response to a call, went out in order and bowed four times, and the beauties of the Six Palaces and the three thousand serving women completed their addresses to the King.

The King and Queen then entered the Inner Halls to discuss palace and national policies. From this time the Queen's majesty and virtue proceeded together, and she was the acme of goodness and beauty. Praise of her resounded through all the land. At this time Sim Ch'ŏng was honoured above all in the dynasty and became 'the Mother of a Kingdom of a

Thousand Chariots'. The King's grace and favour abounded, and in the fabric of affairs there was not a hair-crack of imperfection.

However, Ch'ŏng could not stop thinking of her father for a moment. Two springs and autumns had passed by without her knowing his fate, but it was inconceivable that he was still alive. Day and night she gazed up to Heaven, her brows ever wrinkled with concern.

It was the season of the last month of spring. A Party in the Pear Orchard was being prepared, and the King and Queen were enjoying the delights of the garden at the back, where they saw on the flight of jade steps a beautiful flower arresting the flight of the scent-seeking butterflies and bees, and by the banks of the placid Golden Pond the slender willows inviting the moulting nightingales. Everywhere the spring sunlight glittered and aided man's enjoyment. The King enjoyed himself greatly, and with good wine and fine food composed poems on the changing season. However, sadness suddenly flooded the phoenix eyes of the Queen, and on her brow a cloud of concern formed. She was just gazing blankly into the distant sky and sighing.

The King was puzzled. 'What, my Faithful Queen, in the face of all the beauty of this scene, is the meaning of your face being filled with sadness and your not having a moment of contentment?'

The Queen sighed sorrowfully. 'I was of humble birth and am suddenly come to high and noble position. How can that not be a joy? But there is one deep-cherished thought that I have. Man is created with seven sensory organs, and of them the two eyes are like the sun and the moon. If the eyes are bright, one sees everything beneath the heavens and so discerns all the degrees of good and evil. What is intolerably sad in human life is the blind man. When I think of that — how, though people just like us, they simply cannot see all the beauty of a scene like this — how depressed I feel.'

The King said, 'My Queen, your goodness is outstanding, so these words are not surprising, but, while there have always been the disabled from of old, is there any particular reason for you to feel so sad, my Faithful Queen?'

The Queen appreciated his remarks. 'Your Majesty speaks correctly, but what is in my mind is not to feel such sadness.

What we should do is to assemble all the blind of the capital and the countryside some time, and comfort their hearts with a rare feast of fish and meat. To do this has been what I have wanted all my life.'

The King was unceasing in his praise for her conscientiousness. 'Such a thing would be easy, so why be distressed?' he said, and the next day issued an edict: 'Her Majesty the Queen, out of pity for the blind of this world not being able to distinguish black from white, wishes to assemble the blind from far and near, to give them good wine and a well provided feast, and so to comfort their deep distress. This is an act of rare charity. It shall be published in the capital and the countryside alike that all blind men are to be called and sent up to the capital. If there are any too poor to provide themselves with clothes for a journey, their town is to prepare them for the journey to the capital. If there is any failure to record even one, the regional officials will be dismissed.'

In every province the royal edict was obeyed, and immediately the blind were sought out thoroughly and sent up to the capital. Their number could not be told. The provincial officials compiled books listing the names of the blind and sent them to the capital. Sim Hyŏn too was included among them.

When the appointed day came, the King took his seat in the Hall of Brilliance, and the Queen for her part tried to see to everything. She went round all the Inner and the Outer Halls, and then, after lowering a beaded curtain, took her seat in the Five Peaks Pavilion. The Five Peaks Pavilion's height was lost in the clouds, and its twelve flights of stone steps soared up like a steep mountain, but the careful positioning of the curtain of coral and jewels on silk threads allowed her to see the gathering.

An instruction was next delivered through the Board of Taxation that large quantities of gold, silver and silk cloth should be held at hand. This was to recompense the blind. Then mats were spread on the broad garden of the Hall of Brilliance, the blind were called in a hundred at a time and seated, and tables of food were served to them in turn. Royal music played in the Pear Garden, and the vast crowd of blind men passed round the wine a time or two. Heaven's blessing lay upon them, and they were thoroughly merry too. They all rose at the same moment and danced and sang, 'The Hymn of Peace'. Truly it was the grandest sight in the world, the rarest bounty ever.

They made merry all day long, then were sent home, each with gifts of gold, silver and silk cloth. All the blind men raised their faces to the throne, and cheered and danced their way from the palace. So the feast continued for three days, but there was no sign of Sim Hyŏn. The Queen thought sadly in her heart, 'The whole purpose of this feast was to find my father. There has still been no sign of him, so he must have died.' A silent tear fell without her realising it. The attendant palace girls were curious, but did not dare to question her.

On the fourth day the last of the blind men were brought in. This day it was the blind men from the most distant and remote parts of the kingdom. The blind were coming in in order, and the blind man who came in last and took the last seat was dressed in rags, emaciated in appearance, and could not manage to walk. A servant took his arm so that he was able to go forward to his place, but he had difficulty in taking his seat. He managed to sit down by leaning on his stick. He was all skin and bone, his whole face just a skull. He looked like a ghost. When a table was placed before him, he could not drink a single cup of wine. He fumbled with some food, but could not eat any at all. He was only aware how much of it there was. The whole court was swept with pity at the sight of him.

Suddenly a lady courtier came down from the Five Peaks Pavilion, presented herself, and said, 'Her Majesty the Queen instructs me to call the blind man who is sitting in the last place over there to come below the Five Peaks Pavilion.'

The King thought, 'This blind man is the most outstandingly miserable of all the blind men, so the Queen is trying to show him particular grace out of the compassion of her heart.'

Straightaway he ordered the blind man in the last place to be moved in below the Queen's pavilion. The Ministers went forth and had him dressed in a respectable hat and official robes, carried by a eunuch, and seated on a mat with coloured pictures of dragons on the verandah of the Five Peaks Pavilion.

Meanwhile the Queen had been told that the last of the blind people were coming in. By this time her eyes were sallow and filled with tears, but when she saw the blind man who was in the last place, though he was some distance away and no detail could be seen, by the laws which govern parents and children, how could she not recognize him?

Quickly she raised herself up and sent word to the Outer Halls. As quick as a flash she urged that he come in to see her. A eunuch carried the blind man and sat him on the verandah. The Queen happily looked into his eyes and saw that it was her father for certain. His facial features were all evident, but his skin was so shrunk that he was like a ghost. The Queen cried one word, 'Father', and fell to the ground.

The attendant palace girls went pale with horror and hastily took hold of her to save her. They sent word to the Outer Halls, and the King rushed apprehensively into the Inner Halls and asked exactly how this had happened.

At this the Queen recovered her senses and looked up to see that the King had come near to her and was massaging her hands and feet with his royal hands. The Queen was dazed with awe and hastily arose. She confessed herself guilty of showing disrespect before the King, and her hair not pinned up, but then conveyed to him her inmost thoughts with these words:

'The blind man who is now standing on the verandah is my father. Three years after father and daughter parted, we have now met. The emotions natural between parent and child burst out, and I committed the impropriety of startling Your Majesty. My crime deserves ten thousand deaths.'

When she had finished, the King praised her greatly, saying, 'How beautiful and strange! That is the way things have always been. Yet your devotion to your father, Faithful Queen, moves Heaven and Earth. How can I not congratulate you on the perfect relationship between father and daughter?'

He had a eunuch take the blind man on the verandah up onto the floor of the pavilion, so that father and daughter could meet each other. The Queen stepped out onto the verandah, took hold of her father, bowed twice to him and said, in lament, 'Father, do you not know me, your daughter? I am Ch'ŏng, who was sold to the merchants and was thrown into the Phosphorescent Pool to die. The grace of Heaven being immeasurable, that body is ennobled, and we meet each other, father and daughter. Now, though I die, what regrets should I have?'

She was crying dementedly, and Sim Hyŏn, completely baffled by these words, shouted in a loud voice, 'Is this heaven or earth? Are these things in a dream or in the real world? Are you truly my daughter Ch'ŏng? I mean, how could my little girl who died three years ago become so noble? Has there ever been anything like this? Have my sins been so great that I have no eyes to see you?'

As he said this, he screwed up his face. Suddenly he found to his joy that he could see out of the corners of his eyes. Father and daughter held each other and wept a while. In this place of extremely strict rules they would not have dared to let their personal feelings show as they wished, but the King allowed father and daughter to look upon each other, because no one dead can return to life. He did wish them to let their feelings show just this once. Having this opportunity, the Queen embraced her father and lamented. However, she could not but have regard to the dignity of her position as Queen, and so reluctantly entered the Inner Halls.

She had a eunuch serving man escort her father and settle him in rooms in the rear grounds, and then told the court physician to treat him. In a while Hyŏn recovered completely and could see clearly with both eyes. The Queen's happiness was beyond words, and the whole court gave praise for the wonder of it all.

A few days later the King bestowed upon Sim Hyŏn the title of Royal Father-in-Law, and told him to attend the court. Hyŏn, provided with official robes, approached the jade steps, bowed his head to the ground in gratitude, shedding tears of emotion. 'Your servant's life,' he said, 'has been one of calamity and hardship. I will not go into all the details, but, by the grace of Your Majesty, which is unparalleled in history, beyond my wildest dreams, after three years of separation by death, I thought, I find my daughter has become so noble and honoured, and father and daughter are reunited. It is "a dead tree greeting a spring", "cold ashes blazing into fire again". But most of all, my eyes which were closed are bright again, and the sickness which had penetrated to the marrow of my bones has disappeared like the snow in spring. I have no way to repay all Your Majesty's grace and favours, though I give my worthless life for my King.'

The King gladly allowed him to take his seat, and asked him to tell him the whole story from beginning to end. He heard all that the Queen had suffered, and of her sincere devotion to her father. He felt both pity and admiration for her. He immediately raised the Duke to the office of Second Minister in the Board of Taxation and Master of the King's Horse, with the rank of Premier Duke of the Kingdom. He bestowed upon him a house of a thousand frames and three thousand palace servants. Then he said:

'My Royal Father-in-Law is still not sixty years of age and holds the rank of Duke. He should not be without a wife for any length of time. Therefore, if any officials of the court, civil or military, has a daughter of marriageable age, propose her.'

Sim Hyŏn was greatly astonished. It was presumptious enough of him to have his rank: to remarry was absolutely impossible, he objected strongly, but the King was not pleased to accept this. He said with a laugh, 'The Queen's devotion to her father has been of the highest, and she has made it her first duty to support my Lord, her father, in comfort, never caring for herself. Surely we must respond to such devotion.'

At this point one of the Inspector General's staff made a suggestion. 'Your servant has heard that Im Han, Minister of the Left, has a daughter for whom he has sought a son-in-law for too long. She is now over age, twenty three, I understand, and I wonder whether it might be possible for her to marry the Royal Father-in-Law.'

The King was greatly pleased, and at once summoned Im Han. 'I hear that you have a daughter, my Lord, who is past the age for marriage. How about her marrying the Royal Father-in-Law?'

Im Han replied, 'How could I refuse marriage with the Royal Father-in-Law? Yet my girl is strangely obstinate. From the age of ten I have sought a marriage for her, and she has always said that she would die rather than accept. Many times she has denounced me, and I have got angry in return and dropped the subject. She is already twenty three years old, but, however obstinate she may be, I doubt whether this time she will disobey the King's command.'

The King laughed. 'There is a popular saying that an old

maid is one who takes her fortune as she finds it. Marriage between man and woman is a bond beyond human power. However, when she now marries the Royal Father-in-Law, I shall not fail to give her the appointments due by law and custom. I will bestow on her a high rank, proper to the Royal Mother-in-Law, so how can she refuse?'

Im Han thanked him, returned home and told his wife all that had happened to him during the year. 'This marriage has been arranged by His Majesty the King, so what excuse could the girl find for refusing?' he said.

His wife was only doubtful about the bridegroom's being so old, and was delighted that the girl would have the honour of becoming the first lady in the family of a duke. The girl for her part was sitting and listening, but did not object as before. In fact her reply was so composed that Im Han and his wife were unable to contain their joy, and from that day on prepared the trousseau.

Meanwhile Queen Sim had been giving her father tonics every day from the time they had met, so that the illness which had plagued him for many years was driven away, and his health was robust. He rose to the First Rank of official. Now that, on top of all this, his marriage with a high and powerful family was arranged, she only wished that her first mother were alive, and sighed that father and child, mother and daughter could not be together to see this glory. Otherwise her joy and happiness could imagine no event as auspicious as this.

She was worried that all would not be done in time, and arranged that palace ladies be in solemn attendance on the eve of the wedding, and make the shining insignia and other things for the couple, to be worn on the happy day. When the auspicious time was reported from the Ims' registry, it was scarcely ten days away. The King had the Board of Rites furnish the letters of appointment for the Duchess and the Board of Taxation arrange the trousseau. The Queen furnished her father's wedding clothes, and made the palace ladies responsible for a new set of clothes for him. Not the smallest point was overlooked, and Sim Hyŏn's happiness in his old age was the greatest in history. The love he had received from his daughter was the highest of the age.

When the happy day arrived, the Premier Duke, in full solemnity, set out for his bride's house. The whole court formed his bridegroom's escort. The palace ladies and the high officials bore their staffs and axes of office in solemn escort. It was a thoroughly grand and glorious spectacle.

Sightseers choked the road and roared their praises. 'The bridegroom lived at first in unimaginable distress, but by the love of a daughter he has received such blessings. We see that it is true that "one should not value the birth of a son, but should value the birth of a daughter",' they said.

When the Premier Duke arrived at his bride's house and presented a goose on a jade table, his mother-in-law, the lady Chŏng, peeped out at him from inside the wall, and saw that he was of stern spirit and majestic appearance, haughty and awesome, noble and composed. She was so overwhelmed with admiration at the aspect of this hero of a gentleman that it did not occur to her to have any doubts about his being so old.

The palace ladies paid their respects to the lady Chŏng and prepared the bride in her dress. She ascended into the palanquin, and, with a great display of solemnity, they returned to the capital. In the Pavilion of a Myriad Harmonies they exchanged their nuptial cups with all due ceremony and shared 'the meal of purple mist', as a zephyr filled the rafters. So it was decreed by Heaven.

The palace ladies produced the set of clothes and crown of flowers which the Queen had bestowed, and dressed the bride for court. The bride was tall, and the bright clothes shone brilliantly on her. They added the Phoenix Tail Crown of flowers, which was to her complexion like the moon shining on the sea, so that she looked majestically graceful. Truly she was the blessed mistress of a Duke's great house. The palace ladies and female servants could not but look up at her with adoration.

When the Queen heard reports of this, she had the palace ladies take a thousand pounds of gold and accompany the soldiers. This was in grateful recognition of the boundless salvation of Sakyamuni, because of what she had heard about her former life from the Dragon King when she went to the Water Palace, and by contributing alms in this way she was repaying the goodness of Sakyamuni.

Meanwhile the Premier Duke, in the midst of his perfect glory and honour, lacking nothing now, thought of his old acquaintances where he had been born, and the house in which he had been fed morning and evening. He presented a petition to the government requesting a few months' leave of absence. The King granted this immediately, and the Premier Duke prepared everything for the journey. When he got out on the road, all along his route each town gave abundantly the proper provisions for a travelling government dignitary.

After several days the Premier Duke reached his birthplace and entered his old house. It was a desolate sight, with the eaves broken and the walls falling down, not one to calm a man's sadness. He went to his ancestors' shrines and wept a while.

When he came out, all his neighbours said, 'It is half a year since Sim Hyŏn was put on a horse to go to the capital, and, since we have had no news of him since then, we assumed that he must have died and mourned him. But today Sim Hyŏn has become a great noble, his eyes which could not see are bright again, and here he comes, riding in a four horse carriage with wheels turning like a rushing blue stream, under a red parasol, and his retinue covering the whole road. He comes to take up residence in a house which has decayed away.'

It was Sim Hyŏn, they knew, but the face they knew of old had changed. The people were happy to see this, thought it a miracle, and fought to come forward and congratulate him. They asked for the full story of how his sight had been restored, and how he had come to such glory. The Premier Duke told them every detail from the beginning to the end, and arranged a banquet, to which he summoned all the neighbours.

So the day passed to evening. Candles were lit in the main room, casting shadows on the walls of the two of them facing each other with not a care in the world.

The Premier Duke suddenly thought of past events. 'My life,' he reflected, 'was hard. From the first I suffered as no other. And then what happened? I lost my daughter. For three years my life hung by a thread. But today my daughter is a noble lady, with all this glory, and past events are now become as "a passing dream in spring".'

These thoughts continued to confuse his emotions until the

hour came for the candles to be put out. Then he took his bride to bed. Their love 'soared like mountains, spread like the sea'. When they achieved 'the delight of wind and rain', their hearts fused into one, as if for ever.

The next morning the palace ladies returned to report in detail how pre-eminently graceful the bride was, and how the Premier Duke had found pleasure in her. The Queen was happy, and now that her father and mother were settled at peace in their own quarters, all the pent up grief of her life was dispelled. She continued to care for them morning and evening. The Royal Mother-in-Law was grateful, and the Premier Duke, for his part, marvelled at his daughter's devotion to him.

Meanwhile the lady Im, from the day of her marriage into the royal family, assembled all her household to perform the ceremonies devotedly, and, while receiving visitors correctly, submitted humbly to her husband. She directed the women servants with firm kindness. The household was run with strict fairness. The Premier Duke valued his wife, and, in his perfect joy, thought that every word which the begging priest had said that day long ago had come true.

He got soldiers to take gold, silver and silk cloth to the Temple of the Pointed Rock at the Heart in the Clouds Retreat in the Full Moon Mountains, repaired the temple, and endowed it in gratitude for the grace by which he had been saved. His prayers for long life and prosperity for the Queen must have moved the Gods of Heaven and Earth.

While he was enjoying himself all through the day, the Lieutenant of the County heard that the Premier Duke had come down from the capital. He hastily dressed himself in his official robes, and, with all the proper presents, came to the humble thatched house, presented his credentials, and offered delicacies to comfort the weary traveller. There were mountains of presents: silk cloth, including figured silk and fine silk, and delicacies of fish and meat.

The Premier Duke thanked him. He returned to him half of the gold and cloth which he had sent, and half he accepted to repay fully all the kindness he had received from everyone in former days. First he received warmly the aged couple who had fed him morning and evening, giving them in gratitude gold and silver and silk cloth. The remainder he distributed among his close and distant relations. They were all overawed and would not take them, but the Premier Duke urged them to whole-heartedly. His relations, when they realised how Sim Ch'ŏng had gone to her undeserved death in the sea, and how she had come to life again and become Queen, and how her father's sight had been restored, and he had then become so noble and was now paying a friendly visit to his birthplace and repaying the favours of former days, gave praise, saying:

'We thought it beautiful that Miss Sim went to her undeserved death out of her outstanding love for her father. Now she is so noble and clearly prosperous. From this we know full well that Heaven's rule that the good prosper and the evil are punished is not unavailing.'

There was no end to their praises. The Premier Duke accordingly stayed for several months. He repaired his ancestral tombs, furnishing tombstones, so that they were as well cared for as the mausolea of emperors or kings.

The derelict thatched house, tiny as it was, was the birthplace of the Queen, so it could not be left empty, he thought. He took a derelict room to be the main chamber, and a broken up earth floor as the reception hall, and set up a tile-roofed house of several hundred frames, with the combined efforts of the mayors of the nearby towns. The beams were decorated with pictures, the balustrades were carved decoratively, and the patterned doors and windows shone brilliantly. Wall paintings and calligraphy on the pillars floated in the air. There was row on row of colour-washed walls. It was a perfect residence of a duchess. How could anyone have believed that the former thatched house of a blind man could become today the mansion of the Royal Father-in-Law?

Also in front and behind, and to right and to left, the ground was prepared for agriculture. Several dozen aged female servants were set to keep the house. With the produce of the fields they maintained the sacrifices of the four seasons, and what remained they were to have for their own living expenses.

After having dealt with all matters, he paid his respects at his ancestors' shrines and set off for the capital. The people of the neighbourhood went out twenty five miles or more to see him off, loath to let him go.

So we take the story forward:

In the autumn of the next year the Queen gave birth to a prince. The King doted on him, as if there had never been anyone like him, and called him Yongyun, 'First-born of the Dragon'. He proclaimed a general amnesty throughout the kingdom, and released even prisoners who had committed commonplace crimes. Great was the grace which he displayed and the succour which he gave his people. All the court officials, civil and military, joyfully held a congratulatory session of the court. They shouted 'long may he live' and offered their felicitations.

When the child had passed its three weeks, a banquet was held in the ladies' quarters of the palace, which all the immediate relatives, cousins, wives and daughters of the royal family, were invited to attend. The Royal Mother-in-Law entered the palace this day for the first time, and came face to face with the Queen. After the formal greetings had been completed, the Queen was highly delighted, and without regard for the roles of queen and subject, looked upon the other as her true mother. Her affection for her was so very warm that she talked frankly and intimately with her, respectful in every word and obedient in everything she said. The Royal Mother-in-Law, for her part, without regard for the role of a step-mother, never showed the slightest sign of any lack of devotion. The Queen adored the unique beauty of her face, and admired her obedient virtuousness. She was utterly happy that her father, who had been physically exhausted, by taking such a wife was now not only comfortable physically, but also had a prosperous enough household to maintain fully the ceremonies for his ancestors. Her step-mother's generous and thorough-going big-heartedness were praised, and her inexhaustible love was beyond description. Although the Royal Mother-in-Law observed all the palace rules strictly, she was bright and cheerfully friendly, her voice was calm and pleasant, and at times for extreme concern her words were gentle and loving. It was just as if she had the love of a true mother.

The Royal Mother-in-Law, seeing in one broad first sight what the Queen was like, took no advantage of her, but rather could not but appreciate and follow her. She listened to the details of the hard life the Queen had had in her early years, and was saddened by her sacrifice for love. That day, as they faced each other, and she looked closely at the Queen, she saw that not only did she combine beauty and virtue, but her broad forehead and high nose, her white teeth and red lips, made her strikingly in appearance a reproduction of the Premier Duke. Their voices resembled each other even more. She adored and admired the well-bred talents and virtues of father and daughter, formed an attachment for her in the space of an evening, and loved and respected her deeply.

She stayed that night in a private room, and the next day, when they dined again, a great number of ladies of high nobility, dressed in ceremonial robes, formed lines in order of precedence. Wives of the Three Dukes, Six Lords and all the Barons sat in order. Music of all kinds was played, the five notes and six rhythms harmonising so well as to stop the passing clouds. The singing was enthusiastic, the dancing flowed gently, harmonising beautifully with the Sun and Moon of Yao and the Heaven and Earth of Shun. Truly it was a grand spectacle such as is hardly seen once in an age.

Eventually, at sunset, the banquet came to an end. As the ladies of high nobility and related to the royal family all went to their homes, the lamps and candles blazed and the carriage horses glowed. Sounds of praise were on all lips as they filled the main roads.

The lady felt uneasy about staying many days in the important place, but at the Queen's insistence she stayed a few days longer to raise her spirits. When she went home, the Queen was overcome with distress, and suddenly burst into tears. They promised to meet again at a later date.

So they spent their time in enjoyment, and the Royal Mother-in-Law, ensuring the prosperity and wealth of the family, shortly gave birth to two sons and a daughter, who had the looks of both their father and their mother, and were truly 're-incarnations of young phoenixes'. The Duke was delighted to have children beautiful beyond compare at his knee in his old age, close by him morning and evening.

The Queen went on to give birth to three sons and two daughters. The eldest son was installed as Crown Prince and the other sons each as Princes.

It has always been the way that 'at the height of pleasure

sorrow comes' and 'when all is disaster fortune smiles'.

At this time the Premier Duke suddenly took ill and was on his death bed. The Queen, on hearing this, was greatly alarmed, and sent the court physician. She did her utmost to treat him, but in the end all known medicines were ineffective and he departed the world. His age was seventy five, and it was twenty seven years since he had come to enjoy glory, wealth and honour.

When the Queen was informed of his death, as a filial daughter she moved into a separate annexe, and wailed loudly to Heaven. At the same time the Royal Mother-in-Law lamented until she fainted and passed away. The children, faced with a collapse of their world, could only hold their parents' dead bodies, and, in sad distress at their parents' deaths, be dazed enough to go after them, distressed enough to follow them. The whole household, high and low, wept bitterly in extreme anguish, and their sad laments reverberated far and near. The mourning period was arranged, the Premier Duke was shrouded and coffined, and mourning clothes were donned. The Queen lamented and kept all the rites. She denied herself royal food, and indeed found it hard to keep herself alive.

The King went to pay his formal condolences, and, to console the Queen, said, 'There is no one in the world who will not have to mourn his parents at some time, so why, my gracious queen, do you neglect the state and think only of your personal feelings, go to such excesses of behaviour and neglect your life? Our Royal Father-in-Law suffered uncommon hardship in those years, but then, becoming our Royal Father-in-Law, he enjoyed thirty years of blessedness and wealth, lived to the good age of eighty, and had two sons and one daughter. One may call this perfect happiness, so why do you, my gracious queen, great-hearted as you are, think in such a narrow way, with such excess of mourning? Our judgment in the whole matter is this: perhaps it is all because you, my gracious queen, the most conscientious in the love of your father, were not by your father at the hour of his death, and not able to set yourself at the side of his resting place, finger his dark coffin and weep your heart out. But look: it is said, "It is the manner of women not to rush home a hundred miles upon the death of a distant parent, brother or sister."

So, if this is the case with commoner women, you, my gracious queen, though born of your parents, yet now are the Mother of the Kingdom. Your sense of the dignity of your position is the most important thing, but now you have no regard to your position, and only want to follow your parents. I have never heard that, from of old, a single loving son or daughter followed their parents in death. If you are not ignorant of this, my gracious queen, all this behaviour of yours is deliberate. I want to hear that you are aware of all this.'

The Queen heard him out, and tears fell from her eyes so that she could hardly speak. However, before long she recovered her composure, and said:

'I was orphaned young, and so my judgment is cloudy, and what I have learned has been narrow and shallow. Your Majesty's rebuke today is therefore to the point. I myself am overcome by the vastness of my failings, and only wish the earth would swallow me up. There is nothing I can say to you, but my father first experienced all sorts of hardships, such as few people know. In his last years he was favoured greatly by the royal grace, and his life overflowed with riches and honour, blessings and wealth. But now he has suddenly departed the world. My thinking is this: my father in his last years enjoyed to the full every possible blessing and wealth, except that I, being only a daughter, could not, while he was alive, attend him morning and evening, or perform my duties of wishing him a safe sleep and greeting him when he awoke. Nor was I at his side at his death in return for his precious gift to me of life. After his death I hold onto his coffin, and remember that I could not say my final, eternal farewell to him. I cannot suppress my natural sadness.'

As she finished speaking, she gave a loud cry and wept, and was unable to say all that she wished to say. The King was full of pity for her, and ordered his attendants to give her ginseng tea and meat broth. He urged her to drink them, and the Queen took the ginseng tea and drank it all up, but could not bear to take the meat broth. She bowed her head to the ground and said:

'Your Majesty consoles me greatly, and how could I dare give a hint of my personal feelings against your wishes? Yet since my father's coffin is not yet buried in the ground, at least before his funeral I wish to keep to a vegetarian diet to show lasting sincerity. I humbly beg Your Majesty to pay regard to my trivial personal feelings. If you will, I will feel that your grace is even deeper.'

The King saw beauty in her intentions, and asked the attendants to give her ginseng tea frequently to console her, and so went out to the Outer Halls.

So the day of the Premier Duke's funeral arrived. The King sent officials of the Board of Rites to take charge of the funeral ceremonies, supplying every sort of vessel, and told all the lords to attend the funeral. The magistrates of every district and the civil and military officials of the whole court all sent mountains of condolatory gifts. The grandness of the vessels was beyond description.

The Queen, at this time, could not allay the sorrow in her heart. She composed the funeral address in her own royal hand, and told a palace lady to go in her place and pay her last respects.

The palace lady took the offerings and the address, and went to the Premier Duke's official residence. She conveyed the Queen's orders, and, after she had set up the rite and offered a cup of wine at the spirit tablet, read the address. The document said:

> ' On the date given, Queen Hyosŏng, so named for the sincerity of her devotion to her father, unable to be present herself, sends her palace lady bearing her insignificant offerings, to say her eternal farewell with this short obituary before the resting place of the spirit of the Premier Duke of the Kingdom, Master of the King's Horse, Minister of War, Lord of the Brilliant Fief with the Golden Seal.
>
> 'Ah, alas! Generous was the love and great the virtue of my lord, my father. In my early years he suffered uncommon hardship. Unworthy daughter that I was, I lost my mother at the age of three, and so loving was my father who begat me and brought me up that he took upon himself also the role of mother. His loving labour for me was something very special. Halfway through his life my lord, my father, was reduced to not being able to see the sun or the moon. In a grass-roofed house in the Southern Counties we went through endless hardship, and then, watched over

by Heaven, when we suffered separation by death, suddenly we were re-united in glory. Blessings and wealth overflowed, the best prepared dishes of fish and meat were the least of all we enjoyed, and, with Heaven kinder to us than ever we deserved, his failing lineage prospered more than ever. He had two sons later, and so the burning of incense to his ancestors is continued, and when he departed the world at seventy five years of age, his blessings were unadulterated.

'But what is past is but a dream. I can think of no more to say, but, since I am not as others, I could not attend him morning and evening as I should, I was not at his side at his end, and I could not wish him the eternal farewell on his departure to the Nine Springs of the Underworld. This is something that a child of man cannot bear.

'Ah, alas! Time passes, and now your dark coffin is set for your native place, and you are setting off for your eternal resting place. There is no way for me to express my feelings as I would wish, and I cannot overcome my grief. My palace lady will offer you a cup of pure wine, and tell you that another day I will follow you to the Underworld Springs and meet you again. In the darkness you will understand. Please see the sadness of your unworthy daughter's condition.'

The palace lady finished reading. The black coffin was sombre, the bright banners with his titles fluttered, a sad wind seemed to add to the grief, and the incense smoke seemed to be aware of the desolation of parting. High and low, young and old were all swept by sadness again, and the sound of weeping pierced the heavens.

Now Hŭisŏng and his brother bore their parents' pall down to the ancestral home. The only daughter of the Premier Duke, the young lady Sim Hwa, with a few servants, kept the family home. Her exceeding loneliness and lowliness of state were beyond compare.

Before this, when the Premier Duke's only daughter had been born, not only had his love for her been of the greatest, but, thinking of how the Queen had grown up, he had provided her with clothes and toiletries for all times, not omitting the most trivial thing, and had had her installed in a position like that of the greatest princess of the kingdom, with dozens of serving maids to attend upon her. His love had been without compare.

Now his coffin travelled for several days to reach his birthplace. The day of the funeral came, and he and his second wife were interred with his first wife. Their sons took up residence at the old house, so that they could watch continuously at the grave.

Meanwhile the Queen heard that the cortege of the Premier Duke and his wife had left, and she wailed again. Seven days after the funeral she returned to court, but her heart was full of sorrow for her father, and she kept falling grievously ill. Time passed, and at the third and last annual memorial service for her father she was so grief-stricken for her father that she removed to a separate residence.

After her grief for her father, and because of it, her illness reached a crisis. Finally all known medicines were ineffective, and in the end she departed the world. Within the palace both men and women bewailed her death. All the people of the kingdom thought of her goodness towards them and were as sad as if they had lost their own parents. The King too, when he lost the Queen who had been his support all his life, felt that he had lost both his hands and both his feet. He had no care for affairs, and, as the days went by and he thought of the gentle and generous nature the Queen had had, and her lovely, full, round face, a desperate sickness set in in his heart. Finally the following autumn he departed the world.

The Crown Prince, Yongyun, after bewailing his death, ascended the throne. When it was announced in the capital and the provinces, all the people of the land lamented the death with the keenest distress.

Later Hŭisŏng, the eldest son of the Premier Duke, was one of the three top graduates selected in the King's presence in the civil service examination, and he rose to the office of Minister of the Board of Personnel. The second son, Naksŏng, passed the examination and rose to the office of Minister of the Board of Taxation. The brothers' descendants were numerous, and through the generations the family prospered. This was due to the filial piety bestowed by Heaven and the great virtue given by the Buddha to Queen Sim. Who in the world would not admire her? Virtue such as that of Queen Sim can rarely be discerned, and therefore we must make it our model.

translated by W.E. Skillend

From the Tale to the Novel

W.E. SKILLEND

The idea of 'The Story of Sim Ch'ŏng', that is the basic plot which appears in all versions, is one to catch the imagination, and, unusually for Korean literature, it seems to have no close parallel in other oriental literatures. At the very least, a basically good idea for a story has been worked into many good, distinctively Korean tales.

We should not attempt here to speak for Marshall Pihl, but we feel that his translation of the Chŏnju version, which he has been kind enough to let us see, portrays very accurately a remarkable Korean literary creation. It is bedecked with appropriate references to Chinese literature and relieved with many entertaining, often bawdy episodes. But should we call it a novel? It is largely written in rhythmic prose, and in that respect betrays its origin as a sort of popular drama. In content and style it is suited very well to its anticipated audience, in the market place.

The version we have presented here, by contrast, is unpretentious in style to the point of near boredom, but extremely high in moral content. What, should we conclude, was Ch'ŏng's self-sacrifice for? To cure her father's blindness? That would be admirable, but Ch'ŏng herself clearly did not believe that it had worked when she returned to the human world. To save her father from eternal damnation for having broken a promise to the Buddha? That would be even more admirable, but their extraordinary gratitude — albeit at state expense — to Sakyamuni for having put them to such an ordeal is not entirely defensible by modern standards. The only clear answer the text seems to give us is that such self-sacrifice is justified because it ensured the line of the Sim family, with her half-brothers attaining high office.

The essential unity of this story, its concentration on morality as formulated at one particular time in one particular society, we believe gives this version of the story a better claim to be a novel than the Chŏnju version. Whether it is a good novel or not should be assessed by judgment of how successfully it achieves its own purposes. As to its intended audience, there is no doubt at all: it was the young ladies of the 19th century. The lessons they had to learn are all there: to keep a firm hand on her husband's conduct of his business, to get on well with step-mother or step-daughter, to run a household so that there is no trouble, to be beautiful, and so on. The essential dilemma of being a woman is also very firmly dealt with: after marriage a woman cannot fulfil her obligations to her parents. Her first duty is now to her husband. It is for this reason that no woman can ever be perfect. Only men can be perfect. That is the eternal nature of human society.

However, even Korean society, so carefully regulated for so long, was changing at the end of the 19th century, and the pressures for change which could not be resisted by Korea were those which came from outside, not from inside. Foreign troops flooded in, Chinese and Japanese, and technical innovations flooded in too. One of the latter was the modern printing press. In the country which boasts the oldest piece of printing in the world, as well as the oldest text printed with movable type, but in which manuscript copying had won over both, the huge printing presses of the west came, and the newspaper in Korean was born. And in one of the first newspapers, in 1906, appeared the first modern novel, in serial form.

Its author, Yi Injik, was also the editor of the paper, *Mansebo*, organ of the Tonghak religion, the daily (except on Mondays) vehicle for the patriotic message of that religion. Yi Injik himself had returned about two years earlier from his second stay in Japan, where he had become enthused with the leading role which novelists believed they played in reforming old ways. There were many old ways to be reformed in Korea, he realised, and he took as his model for reform the reformers of Japan. After all, the only choice he had was between reformed, modernised, successful Japan, and unreformed, stagnant and declining China. Since Yi Injik wrote in the years immediately preceding the Japanese occupation of Korea, and even his first novel, 'Tears of Blood', was emasculated under the Japanese as part of the policy to destroy Korea's nationality, Yi Injik has been regarded for most of the 20th century as at best misguided, but more commonly simply as a traitor. Yet we can see his patriotism clearly in the original version of 'Tears of Blood', and we dare to offer it here, since it is most striking the way it breaks with past traditions, in construction, in expression, but above all in motive.

Ongnyŏn's mother is strangely like Sim Ch'ŏng in episode 1 but Ongnyŏn herself grows up, between 1894 and 1902, to be radically different. A new type of Korean woman enters the stage, zealously reforming, with little respect for the old ways. This too is the New Literature, the New Novel in particular, and it was to dominate Korean literature for the next forty years. It was to be the new message that was important, not the medium, and that was the novel, fully fledged at last.

The novel could be read straight through, and in fact it was published as a book, without any divisions into chapters in 1907 and again in 1908, but we feel that it may add something to the appreciation of the work as it was first read if we present the episodes as they appeared in 1906, even down to repeating the editor's mistake of numbering two episodes each 32, 36 and 44.

Tears of Blood

YI INJIK

Episode One (Sunday, July 22, 1906)

With the noise of the guns of the Sino-Japanese War, it seemed as if the whole of P'yŏngyang was flying away. When the noise of the guns stopped, the defeated Chinese troops scattered like falling leaves in the autumn wind, and the Japanese troops swept off like a flood to the northwest. Behind them on the hills and moors was nothing but the corpses of the dead.

Outside the walls of P'yŏngyang, the rays of the evening sun fell on Peony Peak as it slipped below the horizon. A lady stumbled along, gasping for breath as if with the vain effort to catch the sunlight for herself. She was perhaps thirty, and her face was as white as if it were powdered, but in the autumn sunlight, which shone down heartlessly and hot, it had the colouring of a half-ripened cherry. As she hurried along, her bound-up hair worked loose and fell down her back, her clothes worked down so that her breasts were exposed, and her skirt dragged along the ground so that she trod upon it at every step. For all her urgency and haste, she made no progress.

If anyone had seen what she looked like, they would have said that it was a pity that such a young lady should drink and then come out in public staggering drunk. But even if they had said that she was crazy, or having a fit, never mind drunk, such words would not have reached her ears. She was so very distressed about something that, if anyone had questioned her, she would not even have stopped to answer, but would just have wandered on, crying for Ongnyŏn.

'Ongnyŏn! Ongnyŏn! Ongnyŏn! Ongnyŏn! Are you dead or are you alive? If you are dead, let me see your face, even your dead face, once more!

'Ongnyŏn! Ongnyŏn! If you are alive, stop worrying your

mother, and show yourself to me at once!

'Ongnyŏn! Have you been shot dead? Have you been speared to death? Have you been trampled to death? I am your mother, and if I saw a thorn stuck in your pretty young flesh, I used to feel unbearable pain in my own flesh.

'This morning, as we left home, you went in front of me. You toddled along, calling me to come on. Where have you got to?'

She was so absorbed in her search for Ongnyŏn that even if something thought to be ten or twenty times as important as Ongnyŏn had been lost, she would not have acknowledged that. She went on, just calling Ongyŏn until she was hoarse, and then she squatted down, exhausted, on the hilltrack.

(The newspaper was not published the following day, a Monday.)

Episode Two (Tuesday, July 24, 1906)

She was startled to hear someone's voice from the foot of the slope. She listened quietly, and could make out that it was the voice of a man who had lost his way and lost someone, and was struggling desperately.

'This darkness! There's no path here, no path there. Which way can I go to find a path? I am a man, with strong legs, and brave, yet it's as terrible as this for me to spend this night on this hill searching. But my wife's a fearful creature who's hardly been out of the house. What a terrible time she must be having looking for me tonight!'

When she heard this, the lady thought of how she and her husband had lost all trace of each other and got separated in the fighting, and thought that now, by the help of Heaven, they had met each other again. She was so thankful that she shouted, 'Here I am! What a struggle you've had looking for me!' and made down for the bottom of the slope as quickly as she could.

On the way down, she fell on the track and tumbled over, and the man, who was coming up from the foot of the slope, ran to her and took hold of her to lift her up. But when she gathered herself together, she realised that the hand which had touched her hand was a hand like a rope-end, the rough hand of a farm labourer. The sudden shock and dread made her flesh creep, and her heart fell. Waves of fear silenced her.

The man had been going about looking for his woman in the fighting. But when his woman had fled, she must have been wearing a skirt of the coarsest cotton, starched perhaps as rough as chopped firewood with a quart or so of the strongst starch. Besides, his woman was a farm labourer's woman, used all her life to working hard with a hoe or a pestle or a clothes' paddle. He had thought that it was his woman who had shouted from the slope, and come down and taken hold of her. However, the hand of the lady who had called from the slope was as soft as silk, and she was wearing a skirt of almost the finest ramie cloth, which was now soaked in dew. The labourer would have been the sort of man who had never in his life even had a peep at, never mind touched, the hand of anyone who wore clothes like this.

The lady realised that it was not her husband, and the man knew that it was not his woman. The lady's blood ran cold with fear. The man was as excited and as frightened as if he had met a fairy, and his heart throbbed, his breath was heavy, and he could not speak.

The lady had just been feeling terrified about tigers and terrified about ghosts, but now she was waiting for a miracle, for a tiger to eat her up, or a ghost to carry this fellow off. Neither tiger nor ghost came. All she could see was the mute stars of heaven, and here in the hills there were only the two of them, her, innocent and weak, and this wicked fellow.

Episode Three (Wednesday, July 25, 1906)

A person who is afraid for a long time usually becomes desperate. When one is afraid, one cannot breathe properly, but then, if one gets desperate, even a half-dumb person can speak with a flood of words.

'Where have you come from? Answer me! What do you mean by getting hold of a person and shaking her like that? Are you dumb? Are you a robber? If you are a robber, I'll give you the clothes off my body or anything, but take them and go!'

A bold idea came into the man's wicked mind. He was the

sort of person who would not dream of speaking a single word, but his desire was like fire, and the gates opened for a wild flood of words.

'What sort of a wife are you to be out here in the middle of the night? I suppose a wife who's got fed up with her husband and run away. You must be a runaway, but if I seized you and took you to live with me, it would be better than having no wife at all. I think I'll take you. But that'll be later. I dreamt last night that I got married in these hills, and like magic the dream's come true.'

He was a rough fellow, and his wicked words grew more and more terrible. The lady only wanted to die, so as not to see this shame, but she could find no opportunity even to die. Throwing away one's life is the saddest thing one can do, but the thoughts of that lady, who wanted to die but could not, must have been inexpressible. She thought that she should plead with him, and she pleaded with him this, that and every way, but pleading with that fellow was no use, and there was nothing she could do.

Someone shouted from the top of the slope. She did not know what the shout was, but when the lady heard it, she felt as happy as one whose dead parents had come back to life, and she shouted back, 'Please save me!' It may have been a lady shouting, but she put her last ounce of effort into that shout. The vale echoed, and the man up the slope shouted again. It was only a couple of yards from the top of the slope to the bottom, but on a night so dark that one could not see an inch, they could not make each other out, nor could they understand what the other was saying. The man up the slope let off a shot, and the hill echoed with the shot in the night. A crowd of people formed. They were Japanese sentries.

Episode Four (Thursday, July 26, 1906)

It is impossible to say who is fearful and who is fearless. There is no one in the world so fearful as a guilty person, and no one so brave as an innocent person.

The lady felt no fear even at the sound of the shot. On the contrary, she only counted it a blessing that she had escaped her shame. The man had one minute been planning his wicked deeds in his wicked heart, and the next minute, hearing the shot, and thinking that it was someone come to kill him, he was running off.

If it had been broad daylight, he could not even have thought of running away, but it was a pitch dark night, and so, because no one could know if he just slipped away, he ran off without being seen at all.

The sentries seized the lady and made her walk in front of them. They could not speak to her, nor she to them. It was like a dumb man driving an ox.

Martial law was in force where the shot had been fired, and so the military police who were in the neighbourhood of P'yŏngyang all came up. They took the soldier who had fired the shot, and the lady, towards the Military Police Headquarters. She went without knowing where she was, but when a city wall and gate came in sight, she came to herself, and realised that it was the North Gate of the walled city of P'yŏngyang.

It was deep in the night, and there was no sign of men. On all sides hens flapped and cried, and dogs pushed their muzzles out of the holes made for them in the solid gates of respectable houses and barked.

At the sound of the hens and the dogs the lady stopped in mid-stride, unable to complete even the step. She felt as if she were melting away inside, and she was blinded by a curtain of tears.

A dog is a creature with a soul, and one, recognizing someone in the night, ran out thankfully. But a military policeman drew his sword and made to strike it. It was chased away in again and barked. The people could not speak to each other, much less the animal.

'You're guarding the house alone. When we fled, we left you behind in the kitchen. What are you doing out here? If we had stayed at home with you, nothing like this would have happened, but by going to look for somewhere to survive, we've gone onto the road of death and suffering. I've come back alive and seen you again, but I have no husband. And I've no Ongnyŏn, who used to love you. If I had strong legs like you, I'd go everywhere looking for them. But I've no strength in my legs, and the most miserable and piteous thing in the world is a wife. She's afraid of so many things that she can't go anywhere. Hens cry alone in a house without a master, and dogs bark alone in a house without a master. Come on out! Wherever I'm being taken, I'm walking with my feet, but not going with my heart.'

The military policeman shouted for her to move on, and she had no alternative but to be taken to the Military Police Headquarters. The dog followed, barking. The house where the dog had barked, and from which it had come, was the lady's home.

Episode Five (Friday, July 27, 1906)

That was the day when the fighting had been concluded in P'yŏngyang. Everyone in the city had been heartily sick of the Chinese, and that was the day when they had all been chased away, leaving not even a shadow of themselves behind them. It was the day when shot had fallen from the sky like hail, and when it had seemed that all around P'yŏngyang would collapse with the noise of the guns, and that not a single person would survive. The P'yŏngyang people wondered about the Japanese troops. No one knew anything, but tales were told of the fighting at P'yŏngyang in the War of the Year of the Black Dragon three hundred years ago. All sorts of speculations were in the air, and everyone was full of anxieties about the Japanese troops who swarmed in on that day, a solid mass of them, inside and outside the city walls, the way a black cloud floats over the sky in the rainy season.

The people who had been living in P'yŏngyang had been unable to bear the atrocities of the Chinese, and many of them had fled to the hills. But if they met a Chinese soldier in the hills, it was like seeing a tiger or meeting an enemy. What made them feel so bitter was that the Chinese troops would go into the hills, and if they saw a young woman they would rape her, they would steal any money, and even with things that were no use to them they would behave like spiteful children. The people who had fled to the hills found yet more troubles there. So, many of those who had fled to the hills came fleeing back again to P'yŏngyang.

The lady had lived inside the North Gate of the city, and several days earlier she had fled to the hills. However, she had not been able to stay there either, and had fled to the house of a relative who lived in the country. There she had spent two sleepless nights, with him, her, and eight of his family in a single room, and only a few days before she had been forced to return to the city. At that time she had thought that she would rather die than flee again, but today from dawn the noise of the guns had been turning the world upside down, and the rain of fire had been falling among the peaks of the hills and the moors on every side. So they had waited for the dawn and then set off on the refugee road, taking nothing with them, just the three of them, the young couple and their infant daughter, Ongnyŏn.

Inside the walls was a world of weeping. Outside the walls was a world of corpses. In the hills was a world of refugees, mothers calling children, children calling mothers, husbands calling wives, wives calling husbands, nothing but the shouts of people calling those they were looking for. There were people who had abandoned their children and run away alone, and there were husbands and wives grasping each other's hands as they found each other, but at sunset they had all gone and disappeared from sight. Only one lady was left, wandering about, calling for Ongnyŏn on the lower slopes of Peony Peak.

Her husband was Kim Kwanil, a man of twenty nine, with a reputation for spending money freely in P'yŏngyang. They had lost each other in the sea of fleeing humanity, and then Kim Kwanil had come home alone and stayed alone in the empty house that night.

In the middle of the night the dog barked so loudly that he got up and wanted to open the gate and see what it was. However, he was so afraid that he did not open it, but just peeped out through a crack. The military police were already on their way with his wife in front of them, and it never occurred to him that it was his wife who was being taken by the military police, and his wife never dreamt, for her part, that her husband was in the house.

Episode Six (Saturday, July 28, 1906)

Mr Kim stayed the whole night alone in the empty house, sleepless, and with his head full of thoughts.

'On the wide moors outside the North Gate, the corpses of those who had been shot dead, and the near corpses of those who were just breathing their last, were officers and soldiers who had all come onto the field of battle and been killed for their own countries' sakes. They had died in the course of duty, but the young children who had been trampled to death, and the refugee women whom I saw with my own eyes, tripping and falling over them, and trampling on them with my feet wherever I went, as if they were flowers which had fallen in the spring wind, were they unlucky to be Koreans? Did they have the misfortune to be the common people of P'yŏngyang? The land is Korea and the people are Koreans. Are we Koreans suffering such distress in others' wars, as a whale's back might be injured in a battle between prawns? My wife had never gone a step outside her own door. My daughter was a young child of seven. They have perhaps been trampled to death somewhere, and their flesh has gone into the earth, and their blood has formed a stream which has flowed into the Taedong River.

'We should not fail to listen to the screaming of the rapids. Is it not the P'yŏngyang people's voice of lamentation and sorrow? The innocent who are punished are Koreans. The innocent who could not save their lives are Koreans too. Was this heaven's doing or man's doing? Human affairs are most likely to be man's doing. Our people want to think only of themselves. Whether others fail or succeed, they seek to satisfy only their own desires. Whether their country goes to ruin or prospers, the only thing they want is to get on in the world and grow fat themselves.

'The people of P'yŏngan Province have two Devils. One is in Hell, and the other is the Governor, sitting in the Hall of the Proclamation of reforms in P'yŏngyang. The Devil in Hell carries off those who are old or sick or tired of life, but the Governor in his office in P'yŏngyang carries off the healthy and wealthy, every one of them. He is the human Devil and even seems to hold the office of Demon of the Household at the same time, since, if you pay him the proper sacrifices, nothing goes wrong, but if you do not, the whole house suffers and everyone dies. I feel sorry for our people, who cannot enjoy freely what they have earned with their own hands and have mortgaged to others the lives which they were given.

Now, on top of all this, other people have come from their countries and fought and raged here madly. By their impudence we are ruined. All these people have died simply because our country is not strong.

'Well, there's nothing to be done about the dead. The most important thing is to see that the living do not have to face such things again. It is up to us to pull ourselves together. Our country must become bright and strong like other people's countries, so that we, its people, may preserve life and property. We must not allow those vampires, the living Devils and the living Demons, to get into the Governors' offices in every province and all the other local offices. We must see that foreigners do not even think of coming to our country like tigers and bears and having the impudence to fight here. Only then will men be human. Only then will life be worth living. Only then will we be able to treat our property as our own.

'What a terrible night this has been! The people of P'yŏngyang are gone and may be dead. The vampire of a Devil is shut up in some corner. And what has happened to my wife and child? Everyone knew how happy my wife and I were together, and our love for Ongnyŏn was quite exceptional. However, a man with ambitions cannot accomplish great things for his country if he wasted his efforts thinking only of his wife and child. I will set off at once, tour the whole world seeing other people's countries, and get some real education. Then I shall be able to work for my country.'

He waited until it got light, and then left P'yŏngyang for other lands ten thousand leagues away.

Episode Seven (Sunday, July 29, 1906)

His wife had been taken to the Japanese Military Police Headquarters, but everyone who heard how a lady who had led such a sheltered life had suffered such troubles in the fighting, felt sorry for her. As the interpreter translated her story, the Military Police Commander nodded and said, 'Poor thing, what a pity!' He kept her under the protection of the military for that night, and sent her back home the next day. By the time she came back home, she felt as if she had been in that one night through all the troubles the world held.

There is nothing so heartless as an empty house in the cold of a morning. The sight of her home, when she got back, broke her heart again. Would it be worth living alone in her home? She sat down heavily on the edge of the verandah, and then rolled over on to her side, not knowing what she was doing.

Yesterday, in her haste and anxiety to get away, she had not eaten before setting off. For a day and a night her suffering had so filled her world that she had not realised how hungry she was and how her legs were aching. Now she had returned home. There was no news of her husband, and she had no idea where Ongnyŏn had gone. She looked at the four lean pillars, and at the room where the shutters were fastened tight on the empty verandah. 'The best thing would be for this body to drop dead as I sit down here, but if that cannot be, how I dread opening the door of that room with my hand and setting my foot inside it!' As she talked to herself, her voice trailed off, and she gave up caring.

(The newspaper was not published the following day, a Monday.)

Episode Eight (Tuesday, July 31, 1906)

In normal times, neighbours would be coming and going, and the pedlar-women and the cake-sellers would be going in and out, but at that time all the people who had lived in P'yŏngyang had run away at the gunfire, and there were only the Japanese troops there.

The troops wheeled like a flock of crows, and went into this house and that without permission. Of course, on the battlefield, under international law as it applies to wartime, if everyone has fled and houses are unoccupied, it is usual to occupy the houses and commandeer the goods, so if the soldiers saw an empty house, they made a point of going into it. The soldiers who went into Mr Kim's house saw his wife lying on the edge of the verandah, and they just went out again. There seemed to be no one to help her. If she had lain on the verandah for a whole day in the ice and snow of a bitter winter, she would probably have frozen to death, but fortunately the weather was then warm, and so she came to no harm lying on the verandah, dispirited all day.

Not until night did she begin to come to herself, and then she did not come to herself suddenly, as if waking from a dream or a sleep, but she came to herself gradually, the way the mist clears from Peony Peak. At first, when she opened her eyes, she saw the sky bright with stars. Next, when she looked around, she found that she was lying alone in a gloomy house. She did not understand where this was, whose house it was, or how she had come to be lying there.

Slowly she realised that it was her house. Slowly she recollected how she had come and sat down here, how she had gone to the Japanese Military Police Headquarters last night, how people had gathered at the sound of the shot, how she had been all but shamed at the hands of that awful robber, and the thought made her flesh creep all over again.

Suddenly she came to her senses. Suddenly the strength she had lost returned. Suddenly she sat up and thought again only of her husband and Ongnyŏn.

She felt that Ongnyŏn was sleeping in the living room and that her husband was in his room. It was as if she could call Ongnyŏn and she would come, and as if she could call her husband and he would reply.

Surely what she had gone through yesterday was a dream. She must have had a bad dream. Now she was awake and would call Ongyŏn. She turned her head towards the living room and called, 'Ongnyŏn! Ongnyŏn! Ongyŏn!', but as she did so a shiver ran over her flesh, and her voice trailed away.

She stood up and went to the door of the living room. Her legs shook and her heart thumped. She gave the door a jerk inwards, and a noise like a clap of thunder came from the room. She shrieked and collapsed on to her heels.

Episode Nine (Wednesday, August 1, 1906)

When they had fled from this room yesterday morning, nothing had been left lying about, but this morning, when Kim Kwanil had decided to go abroad and had left, in his search for things, he had laid out all their belongings from the storey cupboards and the wall cupboards. He had left all the flaps of the boxes and chests open, and left chests on top of boxes and boxes on top of chests. There were some things arranged tidily, but other things were all ready to fall down. He had had a lot on his mind when he closed the door of the room before he went away, and inside the room he had left the wall cupboard doors and the storey cupboard doors open.

A rat as big as a puppy had come down out of the loft and had had the run of the room, but, hearing the sound of the door being opened, it had jumped down from on top of a box to the floor, and the box had shifted and fallen. It was a box of Ongnyŏn's, and in it were sea shells, bits of tin, bells, and glass bottles. When the box fell it certainly made quite a clatter, but to Mrs Kim in her fear it sounded like a clap of thunder.

She pulled herself together and went into the room to try to find a match. Something caught her feet and bumped her body. She was terrified, and came out again and sat on the edge of the verandah.

She did not know whether it was early evening, the middle of the night, or nearly dawn, and she just waited for the day to dawn. She thought that it must be about time for the night to come to an end, and just gazed at the sky to the east.

Surely that was the first cock flapping his wings and shouting his 'cock-a-doodle-do'. It was certainly hard to pass this night.

A person's anxiety usually grows gradually less over one or two days, but as Mrs Kim passed one day, two days, ten days, a fortnight alone in the house, the bleak, nervous desolation which filled her mind did not grow any less at all. In fact, rather, as the days passed her uneasiness deepened. What reason was there then for her to go on living in the world? Only one thing which she was waiting for was stopping her from dying.

The day after they had fled she saw their belongings scattered about the room, and took them to mean that her husband had been there. She thought that he must have gone looking for Ongnyŏn and her, and, being unable to find them, come back and looked at home, and then gone out to look for them again. She thought of him going about looking for her without knowing whether his baby daughter and his young wife were in difficulties somewhere, or dead, and of how much he must have suffered, and she felt very sorry for him. When the sun set that day and it went dark, she decided to wait in case he should come back, and spent the whole night sitting there without closing the gate. She expected him the next day, the day after, every day, every night, all the time, and whenever she heard anyone's voice, she ran out and looked, and whenever the dog barked she followed him out to see what it was.

She was worn out with waiting so anxiously, and began to lose hope. If there was a rumour that a lot of people had died somewhere, she would think that her husband had died there, and if she heard that a young child had died somewhere, she would think that her daughter Ongnyŏn had died there.

As long as she waited confident that her husband would return alive, she had something to fix her heart on and live for, but when she was in despair that he must have died and would not come, she could not bear to live a moment longer.

Episode Ten (Thursday, August 2, 1906)

She made up her mind to die, and decided to die by throwing herself into the waters of the Taedong River. She waited for nightfall, and set off for the river bank. It was the time of the harvest moon. The sky looked as if it had been washed, and the moon was like a lantern. On the beach, which looked as if it were strewn with silver dust, there was no sign of man, and seagulls were sleeping. She sang a lament.

'Moon, I would ask you a question. You see far and wide.
'I have no news of my husband,
'And I do not know where Ongnyŏn has gone.
'If they were in this world,
'They would have tried to find their way home,
'But they have gone, and there is no news.
'They have surely found lodgings with Death.
'If I live on alone,
'My whole life will be tribulation.
'If I were to die,
'I would not know this tribulation.
'My fifteen years of married bliss,
'My seven years of mother's love,

'When they were I do not know.
'Now they are like a dream.
'This life of mine, like a dream,
'Is only for today.
'The deep green waters,
'That is where I shall go.'

She finished her lament, gathered up her skirt, set her teeth firmly, closed both eyes tight, and jumped into the water. The water was the Taedong River, and the person was the wife of Kim Kwanil.
(The newspaper of Friday, August 3, carried no episode.)

Episode Eleven (Saturday, August 4, 1960)

At a mooring place downstream, a lighter was tied up. In the boat, a boatman and a man by the name of Ko Changp'al who lived in P'yŏngyang, were having a game of ludo together, just the two of them, in the moonlight. This boatman and Mr Ko were not brothers, not even half-brothers, but they were so exactly alike, Mr Ko so like the boatman and the boatman so like Mr Ko, that, although they made their livings in different ways, out of working hours the two fellows were quite inseparable.

What it meant, this being inseparable, was that if only one of them had any money, he would lend some to the other and they would play cards, and if neither of them had any money they had to play something, even if it were only ludo for cigarettes. If they had been told to go without their food for one day, they might not have found that hard, but they were the sort of fellows who would have felt ill if they had been told that they could not have a game one night.

That evening, as usual, Mr Ko had gone to visit the boatman, and they were having a game of ludo together all by themselves, when a strange cry was heard upstream, but they were so completely carried away with their game that they took no notice. However, when they saw that someone was caught on the boat and gasping for breath — the body must have floated down from upstream — they quickly jumped down and fished it out, and found that it was a lady.

If she had jumped from a high bank, whether the water had been deep or shallow, she could hardly have survived, but she had jumped into the water from a sandbank where the water was no more than a foot or two deep. With the water being so shallow, she had not drowned. But since her purpose in throwing herself in had been to kill herself, she remained determined to die even though the water was shallow. She had lain in the water, still alive, and had come floating down until she had been rescued by the men in the boat.

(The newspaper of Sunday, August 5, carried no episode, and the newspaper was not published the following day, a Monday.)

Episode Twelve (Tuesday, August 7, 1906)

The gunpowder smoke drifted away like rain trailing from a cloud. The noise of the guns moved away from P'yŏngyang to Ŭiju, and the rain of shot fell on the White Horse Hill. A bridge of corpses was laid across the Yalu River. P'yŏngyang returned to normal after the fighting, and now it hit Ŭiju.

Imagine that, in a house which catches fire, they put the fire out in the living room, but the parlour catches fire, and that, although the living room and the parlour are both parts of the same house, those of the family who are in the living room congratulate themselves on just having put out the fire in their own room. So it was when it rained blood in Ŭiju, but within the walled city of P'yŏngyang the sound of laughter began to arise.

Those who had fled and holed up somewhere gradually reassembled in P'yŏngyang, and there it was just like old times again. The barred gates of all the houses were opened, and people went to and fro again in all the alleys which they had deserted. Dogs barked, and smoke arose from the hearths. It was a scene of a world at peace again.

But inside the North Gate, at the house of Kim Kwanil, the gate stood shut, and no one came visiting at its porch.

One day an old man came on a pack horse and dismounted in front of Mr Kim's house. When he shook the gate, he found that it was not barred and he went in, but came out again and made enquiries of a neighbour.

'Excuse me, is that Kim Kwanil's house? He's a First Grade official.'

'Yes, that's his house, but it doesn't look as if anyone's there.'

'I'm his father-in-law. I've seen him, and I've come here because my daughter and grand-daughter left home in the fighting, and he didn't know whether they'd come back or not. I just went and looked in the house. There was no one there at all, so I got worried, and that's why I asked you.'

'We left home in the fighting too, and it's not more than a few days since we came back, so we don't know anything for certain, even though they are our neighbours.'

The old man had no alternative but to go back into the house and have a closer look. It looked as if the people of the house had run away at the fighting and a thief had been, the way empty chests were lying about, not in their sets. Then he saw some writing on the wall, the writing of Kim Kwanil's wife. It was her farewell to the world, written on the day when she had gone off to die by throwing herself into the waters of the Taedong River.

When the old man saw the writing, he was taken aback, and the sadness of his heart could not be soothed.

Episode Thirteen (Wednesday, August 8, 1906)

The old man was Mr Ch'oe Hangnae, a man of Chusa rank, who had lived in P'yŏngyang, but ten years earlier, when he was fifty, had moved to Pusan and now had a large trading business there. He was more than comfortably off, but he had no son, and so had adopted one. However, his adopted son did not get on well with him. He had one child of his own, a daughter, and he not only loved her dearly, but he had had a lot of trouble and worry in bringing her up, and she had been very unhappy as she grew up. It was this daughter who was the wife of Kim Kwanil.

If I were to tell the story of the time when Mr Ch'oe was bringing up his daughter, even if I had the tongues of the most famous story-tellers of old, and all the long days of the early summer months to tell my story in, I would not be able to tell more than a small part of it.

Her name was Ch'unae. When she was seven years old her mother died, and she was brought up by a step-mother. The step-mother was praised for all the wifely virtues, but she had one failing, and that was that she behaved cruelly towards Ch'unae, the child of the first wife. If there was anything the former wife had used, even a single dish, she called the shamaness and had it burned or smashed. Only when this was done were her feelings relieved. This was her nature. But one thing the step-mother could neither burn nor break was Ch'unae, the child of the former wife. Mr Ch'oe loved his daughter like a jewel and cherished her like gold, but if he showed the slightest sign of love towards her when his second wife was looking, Ch'unae would be in trouble with her step-mother. So, although Mr Ch'oe often wanted to praise his daughter, many a time when the step-mother was looking he adopted an attitude of scolding her cruelly.

Was Mr Ch'oe then under his second wife's thumb? Far from it! Except for her jealousy of his former wife, who was dead and buried, the second wife was without any fault at all. Even if one made shoes woven of iron thread and wore them to the uppers tramping the length and breadth of Korea, it would be difficult to find such a good wife, was the general opinion in the family. Mr Ch'oe was on the best of terms with his second wife, and, since he also loved Ch'unae, the daughter of his former wife, if he wanted to do anything for her, the best plan was to consider his second wife's feelings in doing it.

Ch'unae was from an early age a sensible girl, and quick to realise how other people felt, not at all like a young child. She would obey her step-mother as if she were her real mother, wiping away her tears. This was the sort of misery Ch'unae went through in her upbringing, and even when she became the wife of Kim Kwanil, Mr Ch'oe could not regard her as a daughter who had left home, but thought of her still as a baby.

When other people heard the rumour of the fighting at P'yŏngyang, they took it calmly, as they might a report of a death in a neighbour's house, but Ch'oe Hangnae, the Chusa, who was living in Pusan, was very shaken and worried when he heard it. Then one day his son-in-law, Kim Kwanil, came to Mr Ch'oe's house in Pusan and told him what had happened to them in the fighting. He told him of his intention to go abroad to study, and Mr Ch'oe gave him funds and saw to it that he was able to go abroad. Mr Ch'oe wanted to know for certain what had happened to his daughter and grand-daughter, and had come to P'yŏngyang, but when he saw what his daughter had written on the wall, the way she felt when she was going to kill herself by throwing herself into the waters of the Taedong River, all the unhappiness his daughter had had in her upbringing came back to him.

He had a vivid picture of when her mother had died when Ch'unae was seven, and of how she had put her cheek to her dead mother's cheek and wept. He had a vivid picture of the way she had been starved of affection by her step-mother. He had a vivid picture of their tearful parting when he had moved to Pusan, as if they would never meet again. Meanwhile the sun set slowly, and as the day darkened the empty house was filled with an inexpressible air of bleakness.

Episode Fourteen (Thursday, August 9, 1906)

Mr Ch'oe called the servant he had brought with him, in a scarcely audible voice that had lost all it strength.

'Boy! Undo the baggage and put it in the verandah room.'

'Where shall I tie the horse up?'

'Take it to a livery stable.'

'Where shall I sleep?'

'Get yourself something to eat at the livery stable, and sleep in the servants' quarters here.'

'I should buy something for you to eat too, sir, before you go to sleep.'

'I'll have something to drink. Bring me a bottle of wine from the baggage, and undo a nest of picnic boxes. I'll sit here by myself in this room and drink, and then at daybreak we'll take the dawn road back to Pusan.

'I used to wonder what war was, but now that I've come face to face with it, I know that the greatest human cruelty is war. My daughter and grand-daughter were my only flesh and blood, and this is how I find things when I come to see them.

'It probably makes no sense to an ignorant fellow like you, boy, but in future, if you want to safeguard your grand-children, you must do something for our country. If our country had been strong, this war wouldn't have happened. My daughter, my child, suffered every hardship in her upbringing, and although she was young and in good health, she has died in the war. My grand-daughter had had smallpox and measles, and had shaken off all the other childish ailments, and she died in the war too.'

'It's you gentry who've destroyed our country. The common people are killed and beaten by the gentry and must just accept it. If they have any property, it's stolen by the gentry. If they have pretty women, they are stolen by the gentry. Common people like me can't do anything for their own property or women, or even to save their own lives. They're tied up by the gentry, so what power have they got to do anything for their country?

'We've only got to say one wrong word and our lives are in your hands. You gentry have got the power to break our legs or banish us. What are the common people's lives worth if the gentry treat us like that? It's you gentry who're to blame for wars. It was one of the gentry, Min Yŏngch'un, who started the Sino-Japanese War by calling in the Chinese, I've heard. Your daughter, the young mistress, and your baby grand-daughter have died because of the war, and their ghosts will get the gentleman called Min Yŏngch'un for it.'

He went on and on like this. Now Mr Ch'oe did not like this servant very much, because he was an impudent fellow, but he had brought him with him because he was a sound fellow to have on a dangerous wartime journey like this. He was deliberately being impudent and rude to Mr Ch'oe in his distress, but this was what happened in a war. You cannot tell them off in a war, and he was so worried that he could not bear to listen to anything at all, so he gave him some money, and said to him,

'Go out and drink yourself sick too, boy. We're so worked up, the only thing to do is to get drunk.'

The servant went out, and Mr Ch'oe sat alone facing the wine bottle.

Episode Fifteen (Friday, August 10, 1906)

He brooded on all his unhappiness and had a cup of wine. He vented all his spite on the world and had a cup of wine. He thought of his daughter and had a cup of wine. He thought of his grand-daughter and had a cup of wine. He got tipsy. He stopped thinking and just drank, then, with his hat still on his head, lay down with his head on a pillow.

As he slept he dreamt. He was fleeing with his daughter and grand-daughter beneath Peony Peak when they met a robber out looting. That was bad enough, but then he saw his daughter fall from a cliff to her death while running away from the robber. Mr Ch'oe tried to beat the robber to death in revenge, but the robber turned on him and beat him back. Mr Ch'oe fell over and struggled to get up, but the robber sat on him, seized his throat and drew a knife. Mr Ch'oe could not breathe as he struggled to get up. Clearly he was having a nightmare.

Someone was beside him, shaking him.

'Father, how did you get here? Father! Father!'

He was surprised by the voice and woke up suddenly. It must be a passing dream, but when he opened his eyes and had a good look, there was his daughter come back alive, after she had written out her thoughts and put her note on the wall, and gone to kill herself by throwing herself into the waters of the Taedong River. This made him feel so happy that he came to himself. But he was not so sure, when he thought about it, that this was not a dream as well.

'My child, you wrote your farewell on the wall and went to kill yourself. How have you come back alive? In my dream just now you fell to your death from a cliff, but now I can see you. Is this a dream, or was that a dream? If this is a dream, I wouldn't mind going on dreaming like this for ten or twenty years in a dream.'

Mr Ch'oe thought that it was really like a dream meeting his daughter, and could not understand exactly how she had really come to him alive.

Episode Sixteen (Saturday, August 11, 1906)

Now when Mrs Kim had fallen into the water and floated downstream, she had been saved by the boatman and Ko Changp'al. Changp'al's mother and wife had put her in a sedan chair and taken her to their home. They had nursed her devotedly for several days before she was restored to health, and that day they had waited for nightfall for her to return to her home with Changp'al's mother. On the way Changp'al's mother had said that she was going to buy something at the roadside and had fallen behind. Since it was her own house she was going to, and she knew the way well, Mrs Kim had gone on ahead into the house. There she saw boxes of baggage on the verandah room floor, and in the living room a light burning brightly.

If she had felt the way she had felt last time, she would not have dared to open the door of the room, but now, after all she had been through, she had no more fear of terror. She opened the door of the room without hesitation, wondering who had come to sit in her room. Someone was asleep there, and looked as if he was struggling in a nightmare. When she took a close look, she saw that it was her own father. She was so glad to see him then that she could not speak, but just wept. Ko Changp'al's mother, who had fallen behind, ran in and did the same.

'Dear master, you here in the middle of the war! We never know what's going to happen next. When you moved to Pusan, I was already old, and never expected to live to see you again, but the old one's still alive, and I am seeing you again. Ah, but the young baby, Ongnyŏn, and the young master have gone away and may be dead. You're here, but they're not here to meet you.'

She spoke as her feelings welled up within her, for she was a very tender-hearted woman.

Now Ko Changp'al's mother was a bond-servant in Mr Ch'oe's family. She had not lived in since she was under thirty, but she had been kept by his kindness. When Mr Ch'oe had moved, Changp'al's mother had wanted to go with her master, but Changp'al was a gambler and had got on the wrong side of Mr Ch'oe, and so they had not been allowed to

follow him, but had stayed in P'yŏngyang. She had felt as useless as a bucket lying in the bottom of a well with its rope broken, but now, thanks to his gambling, Changp'al had been in the boat on the Taedong River instead of sleeping at night, and so had been able to save the life of Miss Ch'oe. So now, it turned out, he had earned praise for his gambling.
(The newspapers of Sunday, Tuesday and Wednesday, 12, 14 and 15 August, carried no episodes, and, as usual, the newspapar was not published on Monday, 13 August.)

Episode Seventeen (Thursday, August 16, 1906)

Mrs Kim heard from her father that her husband had gone abroad to study. She was sad about being so far away from him, but she counted it a blessing that at least his life had been preserved in the war. She gazed at her father's lips as he spoke, and her eyes filled with tears, but her face flushed with happiness.

'Now, my child, the master has left your house, and you can't live here alone, so it will be best for you to follow me down to Pusan and live with me in my house, won't it?'

'I tried to kill myself by throwing myself into the water because I thought that the master of the house was dead and I couldn't bear the thought of living on by myself, but I was rescued from the Taedong River and am alive, and have heard the news that my husband is alive and has gone abroad to study. I can keep this house, and perhaps after a few years I will see my husband's face here again. Don't worry about your daughter, father. Instead, I hope you will be generous in paying your son-in-law's expenses, so that he can study properly.

'I will have Changp'al's mother with me here, and we will be able to live on the rent from one poor field. But if only Ongnyŏn were alive, she would be a consolation to me. How can I wait through all the long years?'

Her words brought a lump to Mr Ch'oe's throat, but he was a busy man and could not stay long, and so after a few days he went down to Pusan. His daughter had Changp'al's mother living with her, so, in the servants' quarters was an old widow, and in the living room a young grass-widow, waiting for

Mr Kim to come back, waiting for time to pass.

Waiting for someone is the most difficult thing in the world, for at night the night is long, and by day the day is long, and the nights and days follow one another and become months and years. Mrs Kim thought that she was the only one in the world whose life was hard. But there was someone else whose hardship was more than hers, and that was her daughter, Ongnyŏn.

Episode Eighteen (Friday, August 17, 1906)

On the day she had fled, Ongnyŏn, not knowing where her parents had gone, had stood beneath Peony Peak, calling for her mother and crying her heart out. A stray bullet flew over and pierced her left leg. She fell down, and only just clung onto life that night on the mountainside.

The next day a Japanese Red Cross nurse found her and had her taken to a field hospital. When the Medical Officer saw her, he said that it was not a serious wound. The bullet had gone right through her leg. If she had been hit by a Chinese bullet — Chinese bullets had poison on them — he said, since it was last night she had been hit, the poison would have spread through her body. However, he said, the bullet which had hit her had been a Japanese one, and treatment would be very easy.

Sure enough, within three weeks she was back to normal, but the child had nowhere to go. When they asked her in the hospital where she lived, she said inside the North Gate of P'yŏngyang. They felt sorry in the hospital for a child who was so young and had gone through so much, and they got an interpreter and told him to take her home. That was after her mother had gone to kill herself by throwing herself into the waters of the Taedong River, and had put her note on the wall. When the interpreter saw the note, he felt sorry for Ongnyŏn, and took her back to the field hospital. The Medical Officer, Major Inoue, was moved by Ongnyŏn's plight, and took a liking to her. He had the interpreter stay and asked her how she felt.

'Don't you know where your father and mother have gone?'

Ongnyŏn shook her head.

'Well, then, if you go and live in my house, I'll send you to school and see that you study. If you work hard at your studies, I'll search all over the country, and if I find your parents alive, I'll send you straight home.'

'If you think that my parents are alive and that you will send me back home, I will go anywhere you say and do anything you tell me.'

'Well, then, I'll send you this very day to Inch'ŏn, and see that you go to Japan on a troopship. My home's in Ōsaka in Japan. If you go there, my wife will be there, and since we have neither son nor daughter, when she sees you she will love you very much. You go and live with her, and think of her as your own mother.'

He asked a wounded soldier who was returning home to take her to Ōsaka in Japan, and Ongnyŏn went as far as Inch'ŏn by sedan chair, and from Inch'ŏn by steamship. Behind her she left her parents, though she did not know what had happened to them, and ahead of her lay the strangeness of a foreign land.

Episode Nineteen (Saturday, August 18, 1906)

If a plain child had been made a refugee at the age of seven and lost her parents, she would have thought of nothing but her mother and father. Every time a stranger asked her anything, she would have burst into tears and broken down, and would not have been able to give a clear answer to the question. But Ongnyŏn was such an intelligent child, and so old for her years, that, although when she was alone she might feel that she would give her life to see her parents, in anyone else's presence she was so normal that she gave not the slightest sign that she was thinking of her parents.

Ongnyŏn's face was like a cut jewel, and so rosy that it might have been rouged. When her parents had made a name for her, they had been so anxious to make a name which would be as beautiful as Ongnyŏn herself that they had very often quarrelled with each other.

The name Ongnyŏn has two characters meaning 'jewel' and 'lotus'. It was her mother who had called her Jewel, because, she said, she was as white as a jewel, and it was her father who had called her Lotus because she bloomed as luxuriantly as a lotus flower.

On the day they named they had disagreed violently, and as a sort of peace pact they had put together the character for 'jewel' and the character for 'lotus' and called her Ongnyŏn, or Jewel Lotus.

Her parents loved this child so much that they thought that although one might find an occasional black lucky stone which looked like a jewel, or yellow flowers, pumpkin flowers, for instance, which looked like lotus, nothing could be found as beautiful as Ongnyŏn, Jewel Lotus. And it was not only her parents who thought so. No one who saw her failed to praise her, and if anyone who had no children saw her, they felt envious enough to steal her. Many a one said that if they could have snatched her away to be theirs, they would have done so.

This was what this Ongnyŏn was like, who had lost her parents and gone alone to a foreign land ten thousand leagues away. Some of the men on the ship would gather round her and ask her questions to pass the time, and those who could not speak Korean would give her sweets from their rucksacks. A young child usually pesters and annoys people, but Ongnyŏn behaved herself.

Episode Twenty (Sunday, August 19, 1960)

The ship, as swift as an arrow on the broad blue sea, reached Ōsaka four days after leaving Inch'ŏn, and there was a bustle as the passengers who were to disembark there all collected their baggage together and got down into the sampans, but Ongnyŏn had nothing but what she stood up in, and she sat alone quietly, and, young as she was, began to think.

'The others are going to their homes, but whose home am I going to? The others all know what they have come to Ōsaka for, and I am the only one who has come to a foreign country by myself, purposelessly. Whose house am I going to, clasping a letter to my breast? What sort of a person is going to read this letter? What sort of a person is going to look after me? If she treats me like a daughter, will I behave as a daughter, and if she treats me like a slave, will I behave like a slave? If she gives me a hard life, will I bear the hardship, and if she allows me to study, will I only study without relaxing for a moment?'

She was sitting, resigned to everything, with all sorts of thoughts going through her head, when the soldier who had travelled with her from P'yŏngyang called her. Since they could not understand each other's speech, she could only see what he meant by his expression. She followed him off the ship. This soldier had been wounded by a bullet in the right leg in the battle of P'yŏngyang, and had been treated at the same field hospital as Ongnyŏn, but since the bullet had damaged a nerve, even after treatment his leg was useless. He could only just manage to walk with the aid of a stick.

He went down first, and as Ongnyŏn looked at him from behind, she said that she had been hit in the leg by a bullet too, but that if things had turned out like that for her, she would have preferred to kill herself, that it would not have been worth going on living. There was no one who could understand what she said. It was fortunate that no one heard what she said, but that was the only good fortune she had. What worried her most was that she could not communicate with anyone. She just followed the soldier, obeying his gestures like a deaf-mute servant.

(The newspaper was not published the following day, a Monday.)

Episode Twenty-One (Tuesday, August 21, 1906)

Everything Ongnyŏn saw she was seeing for the first time. In the harbour the masts of the ships seemed to stand up like growing hemp. In the shopping streets buildings of two and three storeys seemed to tower up to the clouds. A train which was going along like a centipede belched puffs of smoke from its mouth. It made the whole world shake as it went along on its belly, and it raced along as fast as rain before the wind. Her head reeled with the noise of the wheels of the rickshaws going back and forth along the broad straight streets.

The soldier called two rickshaws, and he got in one and put Ongnyŏn in the other. The rickshaws sped off like arrows. Ongnyŏn was only a little girl, and while she had been walking in the road she had taken care that she was not knocked over in the sea of people, and had no thought for anything else. But when she sat up in the rickshaw, again she had nothing to do but think.

'Rickshaw, I want to go slowly. When we come to the end of this journey, I will enter a stranger's house to be fed and clothed, and I am frightened and worried. Rickshaw, I want to go really quickly. I'll only feel safe when I've seen with my own eyes what I'm anxious to know. It may be a good family, with kind people, but it may be a cold-hearted family where the people ooze poison drop by drop. If my fortune is going to be good, they will be good-hearted people, but it is my fortune to be a young orphan travelling to a faraway foreign land.'

At these thoughts tears were beginning to fall like rain, and she was beginning to sob, when the rickshaw came to Major Inoue's house and set them down.

(The newspapers of Wednesday and Thursday, August 22 and 23, carried no episodes.)

Episode Twenty-Two (Friday, August 24, 1906)

When Ongnyŏn saw that the rickshaw had stopped, she guessed that this must be Major Inoue's house. She was so apprehensive that her tiny body seemed to get even tinier. But sadness feeds on idleness, and now her tears stopped.

As she was giving her eyes a couple of quick wipes, the rickshaw coolie in front shouted something, and a woman servant came out, knelt down in the hall, and asked something politely. The soldier said a word or two, and the servant went in. When she came out again, she told the soldier to go in, and he took Ongnyŏn into Major Inoue's house.

He gave Mrs Inoue the Major's news and Ongnyŏn's story, and told her all about the war, while Ongnyŏn just watched Mrs Inoue's expression.

Mrs Inoue was no more than thirty, perhaps the same age as Ongnyŏn's mother. But although she was so near to Ongnyŏn's mother in age, in appearance she was completely the opposite of Ongnyŏn's mother. Ongnyŏn's mother's eyes had charm, but Mrs Inoue's eyes were hard. Ongnyŏn's mother's face was white, but with the freshness of peach blossom, while Mrs Inoue's face was certainly white, but with a cold blue tinge.

Mrs Inoue took and read the Major's letter with cold formality, glancing at Ongnyŏn from time to time. When she spoke to the soldier, Ongnyŏn was sure she was talking only about her, and she sat stiff and straight. The soldier must have said all that he had to say, for he said good-bye and went out. Ongnyŏn was left behind alone in Major Inoue's house, and again she felt the strangeness and awkwardness of it all.

Episode Twenty-Three (Saturday, August 25, 1906)

'Yukiko, I've got a daughter!'

'Your life was certainly lonely without children, mistress, and I'm glad you've got a daughter, but this daughter you've got today is very advanced for her age!'

'You will have to teach Ongnyŏn to speak and write, Yukiko. As soon as she can speak Japanese, I'll send her to school.'

'If I'm to teach the young mistress, am I to continue as a bond-servant? That's what I came to your house as.'

'I'm not asking you to teach her anything difficult, but only to teach her, say, the first year reader of a common Elementary School. Treat her as your little sister, and teach her well. Until she can manage the language, you be a teacher to her at home. It will be hard for you to be a teacher and a bond-servant at the same time, so I'll increase your wages.'

'I don't expect to get any more wages, but I'd like to be allowed to go to the theatre and things like that a lot.'

'Now, Yukiko, take our Ongnyŏn to a department store and buy her some girls' clothes to fit her, and then take her to a bath-house and give her a bath. We'll take off her Korean clothes and dress her in western clothes.'

Although, as you can see, Mrs Inoue loved Ongnyŏn so much, since Ongnyŏn could not understand what she said, she went only by Mrs Inoue's cold looks and her heart fell. She did as she was told as if she were being sent to hard labour.

Even a dog, which cannot speak, knows when somebody loves it, and a human being must surely know even more. Even a young child cannot fail to recognize the expressions of love for it, and so, after a few days, Ongnyŏn, who had even slept curled up, began to stretch out. Mrs Inoue loved

Ongnyŏn more and more as the days went by, and Ongnyŏn became more and more attached to Mrs Inoue day by day.

In the whole of Korean history there is no record of a girl with the intelligence and talents of Ongnyŏn. Korean women are hidden in a corner of the living room and not taught anything, so if there had been a woman as intelligent as Ongnyŏn, the world would have been surprised. However, whatever the reason, there is no Korean woman to be compared to Ongnyŏn.

Everyone who heard of Ongnyŏn's cleverness said that it could not be true and refused to believe it. Within six months of going to Japan she spoke Japanese so well that people who saw her in Major Inoue's house thought that she was a Japanese girl, not a Korean. When Mrs Inoue told them that Ongnyŏn was a Korean child, and that it was no more than six months since she had come from Korea, they said that she was boasting about her, or those who heard that took it as a joke of Mrs Inoue's. But when they got all the details of the story from the servant Yukiko, they gasped such praise of Ongnyŏn that even Ongnyŏn herself could not help feeling a surge of pleasure.

(The newspaper of Sunday, August 26, carried no episode, and the newspaper, as usual on a Monday, was not published on the 27th.)

Episode Twenty-Four (Tuesday, August 28, 1906)

'Extra! Extra! Extra!'

Groups of men ran about past Ongnyŏn along the main shopping street of Ōsaka shouting, as she was on her way home from school, and as she opened the door when she got home, she asked,

'Mother, what are those men shouting?'

'I thought you knew everything, but you don't know what an "extra" is! But something important must have happened. Let's buy a copy and see. Yukiko, go and buy an extra.'

'Yes, I'll go and buy one now.'

She hurried out, and Ongnyŏn ran out after her.

'Yukiko, I'll buy the extra. Give me the money!'

Yukiko laughed, and said that whoever got there first

should buy it, and since her legs were long and Ongnyŏn's were short, Yukiko got there first and bought one. Ongnyŏn took hold of it, asking Yukiko to give it her, and Yukiko could not stop her snatching it. Ongnyŏn took it home, and asked her mother to read it and tell her what it was all about. Mrs Inoue was laughing as she took it. It was an extra edition of the Ōsaka Daily News. As she read the first line she started with surprise, but as she read on a few lines more she gave a cry of pain, threw down the paper, and began to weep silently.

'Mother, what is it in the paper that makes you cry? Mother! Mother!'

Mrs Inoue just wept without answering, so Ongnyŏn, her own eyes filling with tears, called Yukiko. Yukiko was sitting outside the door of the room, and could not see that Mrs Inoue was crying. She could only see Ongnyŏ's eyes as she said,

'What's all this crying for, young mistress, just like a little baby?'

'Yukiko, don't make fun of me! Come in and read the extra, and tell me what it is all about. When mother read it, it made her cry. Read it carefully to see what it says and why mother is crying. Come on! Come on!'

'What is in the extra, mistress? If you've finished with it, I'll have a look.'

Episode Twenty-Five (Wednesday, August 29, 1906)

Yukiko took the paper and looked at it with a broad smile. She did not read very far down or very carefully before she began to speak.

'Mistress, look at this! The Liaotung Peninsula has surrendered. Isn't it marvellous the way Japan wins every battle? Oh my goodness, such a lot of our soldiers have been killed! Mistress, what's this? The master has been killed! They told us that there is no danger where the Red Cross flag is flying on a battlefield — that's international law — but the master was a medical officer, and he's been killed. How can it have happened?'

'What? Father's been killed?' Ongnyŏn shouted, and she began to cry. Mrs Inoue just wept silently, and Yukiko's lips quivered as she looked at Mrs Inoue. The whole house was filled with weeping. One 'extra' had shattered the happiness of the whole house.

Major Inoue had gone along the road along which man never returns, and Mrs Inoue passed the time alone in an empty room with a cold pillow.

According to Korean custom, it is regarded as the finest thing for a young widow not to remarry, and her life is nothing but care. But since there is no such evil custom — moral crime, one might call it — in civilised countries, there is no shame anywhere else in the world in a young widow marrying again. So Mrs Inoue found a good man to marry.

'Ongnyŏn, I am young and cannot live by myself all my life. I am going to get married, but the trouble is that there's no one to take care of you.'

All Ongnyŏn wanted was to go with her foster-mother when she got married, but when Mrs Inoue said that she could not take her with her, Ongnyŏn felt that there suddenly came over her again the heartbreak she had suffered when she had lost her parents at the foot of Peony Peak outside the walls of P'yŏngyang.

(The newspaper of Thursday, August 30, carried no episode.)

Episode Twenty-Six (Friday, August 31, 1906)

Ongnyŏn curled up on Mrs Inoue's knee, and her voice choked as she said,

'Mother, if you leave me, who will I have?'

'There, there. The only thing you can do is to take it as if I had died.'

'If you die, I'll die with you!'

Mrs Inoue's heart missed a beat as Ongnyŏn said this, and she went off into thought. She had told the marriage broker that she was alone, and that was what her husband-to-be understood, so now it would be difficult to change her story and tell him that she had a daughter. But, on the other hand, when she saw how attached Ongnyŏn was to her, she could not bear the thought of abandoning her.

'All right, Ongnyŏn, don't cry! I won't get married, and that's an end of it. I'll stay here and see that you go to school, but in another ten years I'll have to depend on you, so study hard.'

'Will you really not get married, mother? Will you stay here and see that I go to school?'

'Now don't worry! Would I lie to a young child?'

When Ongnyŏn heard this, the happiness in her heart was too much for her. She sat on Mrs Inoue's knee, put her cheek to hers, and cuddled her as a baby would.

From then on Ongnyŏn was more attached to Mrs Inoue than ever. When she went to school, her only wish was to get home again. At school dismissal time she would run home and throw her arms around Mrs Inoue and cuddle her.

But it was not many days before Mrs Inoue began to look displeased at this cuddling. At first she had been very happy to be cuddled by Ongnyŏn, but then for some reason she began to get cross with her for doing it. She became cool towards Ongnyŏn, and as the days went by Ongnyŏn felt more and more that her life was a journey of unhappiness and sorrow.

When Mrs Inoue had been going to get married, she had given up the idea out of pity for Ongnyŏn's situation, but every time the young woman felt lonely in her empty room, she felt that she hated Ongnyŏn.

Even if a woman's child is one born of her own womb, and not a child she has got from somewhere else, it seems that any feelings of annoyance she has towards it grow day by day.

Episode Twenty-Seven (Saturday, September 1, 1906)

While Ongnyŏn had been loved by Mrs Inoue, she had not liked the thought of going out of the house, but when she began to be hated by Mrs Inoue, once she left the house she did not like going back. Mrs Inoue, while she had loved Ongnyŏn, used to wait at the door if Ongnyŏn went out anywhere and was late coming back, but when she came to hate her, if she saw her coming, she would glare at her, and wonder what this enemy coming into her house had to do with her.

Sitting or standing, eating or sleeping, Ongnyŏn was under this glare of hatred. She grew up under this glare, and became more and more conscious of Mrs Inoue's expression. She often wept.

Three years passed, every day of them like three years. Ongnyŏn had gone to the Common Elementary School and was in her fourth year. At the school leaving ceremony she was top of the whole school, and therefore praised by everyone. But when she heard the praise, it did not make her happy in the least. In fact not only did it not make her happy, but it even hurt her to hear it.

Of all the things she hated to hear, the worst was this sort of thing:

'They say she's Major Inoue's adopted daughter. I believe the Major was killed at the time of the surrender of the Liaotung Peninsula, and his wife didn't even get married again because she felt sorry for her foster-child Ongnyŏn.'

'Goodness, I do admire her! D'you think that young Ongnyŏn realises how kind she has been?'

'Realises? Never! Other people's children are no good. It's an admirable thing to have done. You won't find many like Mrs Inoue to bring up somebody else's child and see that she goes to school, instead of getting married while she's still young.'

Everyone at the school leaving ceremony flattered Ongnyŏn for her ability, but when they began to praise her foster-mother, going on and on, back and forth between each other without stopping, every word filled Ongnyŏn with a sorrow which no one else could understand.

Episode Twenty-Eight (Sunday, September 2, 1906)

Ongnyŏn came back home, opened the door and went in.

'Mother, I've got my school leaving certificate.'

'Now that you've finished your studies, you must keep your mother. *Your* studies, indeed! If I hadn't seen to it that you went to school, what education would you have had? If you'd grown up in Korea, you wouldn't even have had a look at a school book! It was your good luck that the war with China broke out. You were lucky, But I was unlucky. I've gone through a lot for a long time, just to see that you went to school.'

As Mrs Inoue's self-righteousness poured out, Ongnyŏn lowered her head and thought to herself that a girl who had only finished elementary school could not keep Mrs Inoue, and she did not want help from Mrs Inoue to continue at school. There was only one thing for it, she thought. She would throw away her life as soon as possible, and so get out of Mrs Inoue's sight. She would go to join the dead this very day, and so meet her parents who had died in the war. She made up her mind, but gave nothing away by her expression as she answered Mrs Inoue properly.

That night she went down to Ōsaka harbour, determined to kill herself by throwing herself into the water.

There were a lot of people down at the harbour, so she went to look for some deserted place. There was a faint moon, so that one could recognize anyone nearby, and wherever she went there were people. She went to the east, turned round to the west, turned round again, and the way she kept wandering about must have looked very suspicious.

Someone called from behind her, 'Hey! You there!', and when she looked round she saw that it was a policeman. She jumped and was too taken aback to answer quickly, which made the policeman even more suspicious. He came up to her and questioned her. Ongnyŏn, forced to make some reply, said that she had gone out to the market to buy something, and had got lost, and was trying to find her way home. The policeman forgot his suspicions and asked her her address. He took her home, and told Mrs Inoue Ongnyŏn's story of her being lost. Mrs Inoue thanked him, and after seeing him out, called Ongnyŏn to come into her room and sit down. She questioned her.

'What made you go out to the harbour tonight? He said you went east, west, north and south, wandering over the whole of Ōsaka. What did you go out for, unless you're mad, of course? I could easily be disgraced by a daughter like you. That's just the sort of thing the papers thrive on.'

Ongnyŏn listened to this sort of scolding until her head was bursting, but, since she had quite made up her mind, she could feel no more sadness, and she just waited for the next night. (The newspaper was not published the following day, a Monday.)

Episode Twenty-Nine (Tuesday, September 4, 1906)

That night Mrs Inoue felt lonely and sad, and could not sleep. She went to bed, but got up again, lit again the light which she had put out, and started to read a novel. Soon she put the book down and sat apparently brooding listlessly. The old woman, who had gone to sleep by the door, was awakened and got up. She said,

'Mistress, why have you got up again after going to bed?'

'When fate is cruel and one has a lot of cares, can one sleep easily?'

'What's the use of complaining about your fate, mistress? Even now, if you're sensible, it can be all right. Isn't it only for the sake of the young mistress that you've been through such a lot on your own up to now?'

'Yes, you're right. I've been a fool to go through all this for the sake of somebody else's child.'

'Yes, you wouldn't mind if the young mistress was grateful to you, but far from being grateful, when she looks at you she just glares slyly, and you can see that she loathes you.'

'Yes, you're right. Just for her I didn't get married when I had the chance, and I've suffered for three or four years. However young she may be, you'd think she'd be grateful, but that one's got no manners at all. Just look what happened this evening. What a strange thing to do, wasn't it? What could such a young thing have meant to do, going out to the harbour in the middle of the night? Perhaps she meant to kill herself, to throw herself in the water. I don't know. Have I been so cruel to her that she's unhappy enough to try to kill herself? It's quite beyond me. If she killed herself, everyone would think that I'd ill-treated her. Have I done anything wrong like that?'

'To kill herself? Never! If she'd been going to kill herself, she'd have gone somewhere where no one could see her do it. Wandering about the whole of Ōsaka like that, this way and that, wasn't a policeman bound to spot her? She only did it to give you a bad name. It's no use your staying single, going through all this, mistress. If you want to get married, you must do it at once, before you're a year older. Look at me! I'm fifty, and my hair's turning grey. I didn't realise that I was growing old. There's nothing so cruel and sly as the way time passes.'

'Everyone grows old like that. Can I avoid it, and stay looking like this all my life? If I could find someone to marry, going just by myself, so that I'd have no trouble, I'd find myself a husband tomorrow, or the day after.'

(The newspaper of Wednesday, September 5, carried no episode, and the newspaper was not published the following day, Thursday, September 6.)

Episode Thirty (Friday, September 7, 1906)

Mrs Inoue and the old woman may have thought that Ongnyŏn was asleep as they talked, or they may not have cared whether she was asleep or not, nor whether she heard or not. Anyway Mrs Inoue made up her mind to abandon Ongnyŏn and get married, she was saying.

Ongnyŏn, who had gone out that night to kill herself by throwing herself into the water, and had come home without having been able to do so, because she had been caught by the policeman, was sleeping near Mrs Inoue. She had swallowed what she wanted to say and wept, and dropped off to sleep for a while.

She had a dream.

She had wanted to kill herself, and had gone out and was making for the Taedong River, but was unable to walk. In sight of the river, she had been unable to get to it, and was struggling with all her might to do so when suddenly she heard a voice calling 'Ongnyŏn! Ongnyŏn!' from behind her. When she looked round, she saw that it was her mother. She did not feel especially happy to see her, and said, 'What are you doing here? I've come here today to kill myself by throwing myself in the water.'

Her mother said, 'Don't kill yourself, my dear. Your father's sent a letter to say that he wants to see you.'

As her voice trailed away, Ongnyŏn woke up to find herself near Mrs Inoue, just as the old woman was saying, 'Mistress, why have you got up again after going to bed?' Ongnyŏn thought how nice it would be to go back to sleep and continue the dream, but when the two women went on to talk to each other, back and forth, just about her, she suddenly became wide awake, and all thought of sleep and of continuing her dream vanished. She lay with her back to the light, and what she heard made her heart ache.

The old woman was only talking to make Mrs Inoue feel happier, and Mrs Inoue somehow came to feel so close to the old woman that night that she said to her that wherever she went, she would take the old woman with her, she could be sure of that. The old woman replied,

'Mistress, why go to any husband's house? Your husband can come here. Don't go to get married, let's tell your husband to come here and marry you. You have property and a good house like this, so whether your husband has property or not, as long as he's a good-hearted man, it will be all right. Just get rid of the young mistress, that's all. But let me stay with you until I die, and don't treat me badly.'

Episode Thirty-One (Saturday, September 8, 1906)

Mrs Inoue told her to bring a bottle of wine, and said,

'Listening to what you say makes me feel better, and seems to chase away all my worries. Do you think that I could be so heartless as to treat you badly? Have a drink before you go to sleep.'

The two of them drank glass after glass of wine until the bottle was empty, and then lay down, and obviously fell into a deep sleep. As the clock struck three in the morning, the old woman's snores were making the ceiling ring.

Ongnyŏn got up and sat quietly for a while. Glaring at the old woman she said,

'You wicked old fox, how many people have you caught and eaten to feed yourself up to now? I hate the sight of you. I will soon die, but I hope you'll live for a good hundred years more with your ugliness.'

Then, turning her head, she looked at Mrs Inoue and said,

'It was my P'yŏngyang father and mother who created my body, and it was my father Inoue and my Ōsaka mother who saved my life and brought me up. It was because my stars were unlucky that I lost my parents in the war. So, young and weak as I was, I was able to bear life in this far distant land only by trusting in my Ōsaka mother. I have had such kindness from you, but it is because of me that you are worried and in trouble. It is all Ongnyŏn's fault.

'As long as I live, I cannot repay your kindness. If I kill myself straightaway, without waiting a day or an hour, I'll stop being a worry to you, and I will forget my own cares too. I am going, mother. I hope your life will be free of care.'

She cried, calmed down after a while, got up, and opened the gate and went out. The road on which she was going was the road to the grave.

She ran to the harbour. The place she was making for was where the broad deep sea seemed to touch the sky. She gazed at the water and said,

'Ah, I am glad to see you. I am going back the way I came. When the war broke out, our family seemed to face it alone. I don't know where my parents died. I was hit by a bullet, and would have died, but my life was saved by Major Inoue, and I came here across the sea in a troopship. I came on the sea, and I will go in the sea.'

Episode Thirty-Two (Sunday, September 9, 1906)

'If I throw myself into the water, I hope my body will not rot in the water, but will bob away with the waves and wind, past Kōbe and Shimonoseki, in front of Tsushima, seeing the Korea Straits, going as swiftly as an arrow until it enters Chinnamp'o Bay. Then, if it goes upstream, up the lower reaches of the Taedong River, I will see the North Gate of P'yŏngyang, and if my body does rot, I hope it will rot in the Taedong River. Water, answer my prayer! I trust you to take me.'

The sea murmured as if in reply to her words, and the whole world seemed to be lost in the sound of the water. Ongnyŏn went dizzy with it, and fell over.

Her mind was full of sorrow and sadness, and she was stunned for a moment. As her strength returned a little, she slept, and she had another dream.

She could hear someone calling 'Ongnyŏn! Ongnyŏn!' from behind her. She could not see anyone, but she thought it was her mother. The voice said, 'My dear, don't kill yourself — let's meet once more!' She made a valiant effort to reply, but could not make a sound. she put every ounce of effort into it, and she opened her eyes and saw the sky full of stars. The sea was murmuring as before. She was in a dreamy state as she came out of her faint or sleep or whatever it was. She thought, 'I have had two dreams tonight in which my mother has told me not to kill myself,' and she began to wonder whether her mother might not be alive. She began to sort things out a bit, and followed this new line of thought.

'My mother must be alive and wanting to see me again before she dies, because heaven has been moved and the spirits have taken notice, and she has appeared in my dreams. If I kill myself, I am an unfaithful daughter to my parents. If hardship comes my way, the correct thing is to bear it, and if I have cares, the correct thing is to forget them. Yes, from the age of seven until now I have lived in hardship, so I shall not kill myself. I shall stay alive, and not die until I see my parents' faces once again.'

She turned round and went into Ōsaka again.

(The newspaper was not published the following day, a Monday, and the issue of Tuesday, September 11, carried no episode. The next episode was again numbered 32.)

Episode Thirty-Two (Wednesday, September 12, 1906)

The day was just dawning as she hurried to Major Inoue's house. She did not go in, but stood outside and listened quietly. She heard the old woman's voice.

'Mistress, mistress, where has the young mistress gone?'

'Mm? what's that? I dozed off and I've only just woken up. Where's Ongnyŏn gone, did you say? Perhaps to the lavatory. Call her.'

'I've just been to the lavatory myself. I'd latched the front gate inside, but it's open now. She must have gone out.'

When she heard this, Ongnyŏn felt that she could not go in, and she turned round and went off, though she had nowhere to go. She went unthinkingly towards the station, just as the passengers for the early morning train were pouring in. She wanted to go perhaps to Tōkyō or somewhere like that, but she did not have enough money for a ticket to Tōkyō. She had only twenty sen, but she was determined to get away from

Ōsaka wherever she went, and to earn her keep in somebody's house. So she bought a ticket for Ibaragi, and got on the early morning train.

There were too many people in the third class coach, and Ongnyŏn could not find a seat and had to stand. From behind her she heard a young man grumbling to himself in Korean, 'There's some girl standing in front of me.' When Ongnyŏn looked round, she saw that he was seventeen or eighteen, with a face the colour of a peach ripened in the sun, a fine handsome nose, and eyes full of life. He was dressed in western clothes, but so badly that it must have been the first time he had worn them. When he saw Ongnyŏn turn round, he said to himself, again in Korean,

'What a fine girl! She's clever, I'm sure. If you take our Korean girls, girls like her just idle away all their time, but here girls like her all go to school, I believe. I wonder what she is.'

Episode Thirty-Three (Thursday, September 13, 1906)

None of the people round about understood what he was saying, but Ongnyŏn not only understood, but, since this was the first time she had heard her native language spoken in all the years since she had come to Ōsaka, her happiness knew no bounds. She was only a girl, and too polite to speak first. Without addressing him, she too spoke to herself, but just loudly enough for the young man to hear.

'I must find somewhere to sit. I can't stand all the way.'

The young man behind her was surprised to hear this.

'Is she a Korean? I took her for a Japanese, but she spoke Korean!'

He asked her without any further ado,

'Are you a Korean, my girl?'

'Yes, I am.'

'Oh! How old are you, and how long have you been here?'

'I was seven when I came here, and I'm eleven now.'

'What have you been doing since you came here?'

'I've been to a Common Elementary School, and yesterday was the day I finished there.'

'You're doing better than me! I'm just setting off for

America for my education, but in America they speak a different language and their writing is different, and when I go there not knowing a single letter or a single word, what an awful time I'm going to have! You say it's four years since you came to Japan now, so you'll have left all that behind you. It's a very fine thing for a young child to come all this way to go to school.'

'At first when I came, all I wanted to do was to learn, and I didn't mind when people praised me, but now my luck's changed, and here I am on the road of trouble. Now if people praise me . . .'

Her voice choked in her throat, tears welled up in her eyes, and she lowered her head quickly. The young man stared at her, and they said nothing to each other. The whistle blew in the station and the train pulled out, puffing great black clouds of smoke from its funnel.

Ongnyŏn would have to get off when they got to Ibaragi, and she wondered what sort of family she would have to go to, and what sort of a life she was in for. The future was so uncertain. If she had been wanting to get to Ibaragi, the journey there would have seemed very slow, but since that was as far as her ticket would take her, and she would have to get off there whether she liked or not, the way the train was racing along so perfectly, it seemed as if it would reach the edge of the world by nightfall. And Ibaragi was no distance at all.

The young man spoke to her. 'I don't know where you're going, but if you stand all the way, your legs are going to be aching, aren't they?'

'I'm only going as far as Ibaragi.'

'Is there someone you know in Ibaragi?'

'No, no one.'

'Why are you going there then?'

Ongnyŏn wiped her eyes with a handkerchief and did not reply. The young man wanted to ask her more, but since all the people round about were taking an interest in them, he pretended indifference to her, and put his head out of the window and gazed at a mountain in the distance. But all he could think of was Ongnyŏn's eyes filled with tears.

(The newspaper was not published the following day, Friday, September 14.)

Episode Thirty-Four (Saturday, September 15, 1906)

The train, which had been racing, gradually slowed down, and then stopped with a jerk. As it jerked backwards, Ongnyŏn, who had been standing, fell over. She grabbed at the young man's knee with her hand, and accidentally made his leg jump as she hit his knee. He had been sitting just looking out of the window, but this made him look round in surprise. Ongnyŏn said that she was sorry, speaking in Japanese without thinking. Since the young man knew no Japanese, he could not understand her, but he could tell that she was saying that she was sorry by her expression, and he went straight on as if nothing had happened.

'Is this where you're going?'

As he said this, the conductor came along shouting, 'Ibaragi! Ibaragi! Ibaragi! Ibaragi!' and when he opened the door, Ongnyŏn, whose young body was steeped in Japanese custom, bowed to the young man from the waist, said good-bye to him, again in Japanese, and got off the train.

The air was filled with the noise of wooden clogs as the passengers poured on and off the train, and the young man, who was in a state of some confusion, tried to spot Ongnyŏn as she went away. He looked out of the window, but she was soon lost in the crowd and he could not see her. He picked up his case and went out after her.

Ongnyŏn was surprised to meet him at the exit, and she went out without saying a word. The young man followed her without saying anything either.

Ongnyŏn made her way out of the station, but since she did not know where to go, she started off rather aimlessly. A rickshaw coolie, with a glint in his eyes of some money to be made, ran after her, asking her to take his rickshaw. But Ongnyŏn, who had no money, and did not know where to go, stood there without giving him a glance.

The young man spoke to her.

'Look, I'd like to ask you a favour. I've only just come to Japan. I've never been here before, and I want to ask you some things. Would you mind dropping into an inn for a little while?'

'All right. There's a travellers' rest over there. We can go in, and you can tell me what you want to tell me.'

She went on ahead. Neither she nor the young man had ever been in Ibaragi before, but Ongnyŏn went into the inn with all the assurance of someone who had been to Ibaragi many times.

Episode Thirty-Five (Sunday, September 16, 1906)

A servant led them up to the highest room in the three storey building, and went down again. This was the first time the young man had ever seen anything like this. He was quite lost, and thought it a great stroke of fortune that he had met Ongnyŏn.

'You know, I've only got as far as here and you see how helpless I am. What am I going to find things like when I get to America? You've been abroad for a long time, and I'm sure you know your way about very well. So there's a lot I can learn from you for a start. Now that we've met like this by chance so far from home, let's not separate without at least telling each other what we're doing.

'I'm Ku Wansŏ. I wanted an education, so I left Korea to go to America without telling my parents. But I've got no further than this before I feel so helpless, and I don't know what to do for the best.'

As he went on like this, Ongnyŏn felt as if it were not just any fellow-countryman she had met, but one of her family. She told him all her story in every detail, from the day she had cried her heart out at the foot of Peony Peak to the day when she had tried to drown herself in Ōsaka harbour.

'If that's the way things are, let's go over to America together. We can to go school, and if you get any news of your parents, I'll let you go home to Korea before me.'

Ongnyŏn seemed doubtful, so he went on.

'Now don't worry about school fees. Look, we are Koreans. What use are our lives if we don't study and get away from barbarism? I believe you think that you were the only one affected by the Sino-Japanese War, but it affected every one of our people. People who say "Everything's all right. Nothing happened to me. I didn't see anything" are weevils. If everyone takes that attitude and lives without a thought for the rest of the world, in another few years' time there's going to be another war like the Sino-Japanese War in our country. You must start studying now, without wasting a day. Then it will be up to you to undertake the education of the women of our country and open the road to civilisation.'

When he said this, all the cares which had been crowding Ongnyŏn's mind disappeared as if they had been swept away, and the two of them went straight to Yokohama and boarded a ship. On the broad waters of the Pacific . . .

(The newspaper was not published the following day, a Monday.)

Episode Thirty-Six (Tuesday, September 18, 1906)

The steamer raced on night and day as straight as an arrow, bobbing like a cork, and in three weeks reached San Francisco. When they dropped anchor, there they were in America. When it was daytime in Korea, it was night in America, and when it was night in America, it was daytime in Korea. It was a completely different country, where day and night were reversed. The country looked unfamiliar, and it was the first time they had seen people like the Americans. They were tall, with long noses, yellow hair and white skins. They might have been bursting with good-heartedness, but Ongnyŏn was terrified at the sight of them.

Mr Ku and Ongnyŏn did not know where to go when they went ashore, and they had a long discussion.

'Ongnyŏn, can you speak English? Not even a little? Not one word? Well, we're in a fine mess then. We can't ask our way about!'

Tall buildings of four or five storeys seemed to reach right up to the clouds in the sky. The way seething crowds of people were going in and out made it seem that many of the buildings were inns, but since they could not speak the language, the young pair did not know what to do for the best. Ongnyŏn picked on a passer-by and asked a question in Japanese. Mr Ku thought that Ongnyŏn did know a little English, and had only said that she did not out of modesty. He stepped close up to her to listen to the words which he could not understand.

The lady Ongnyŏn addressed was so tall that it seemed that even two Ongnyŏn's standing one on top of the other would have to look up at her. She was wearing something like a bird net on her face, and she had with her a young child who looked as crisp and clean as a radish root. When Ongnyŏn spoke to her as she passed by, she must have said, 'What did you say?' but to Mr Ku and Ongnyŏn it sounded just like gibberish, not like someone speaking a language at all. The lady turned to a man in a frock coat behind her and babbled something else. The man was a westerner who could speak Chinese, and he said something to them in Chinese, but this too sounded like gibberish, not like speech, to Mr Ku and Ongnyŏn. Mr Ku thought Ongnyŏn could understand.

'What did he say, Ongnyŏn?'

'I'm afraid I don't know.'

'Didn't you understand what he said either?'

(The next episode was again numbered 36.)

Episode Thirty-Six (Wednesday, September 19, 1906)

The situation was getting worse and worse, when a group of Chinese labourers passed by. Mr Ku ran after them and tried to start a conversation in writing with them, but there was no one among the labourers who knew how to write Chinese. They covered their eyes with their hands and then lifted their hands up again and waved them about to show that they were illiterate and could not read.

Just at that moment a Chinese, dressed in silk clothes which glinted in the sunlight, passed by in a coach which was being driven like the rain before the wind. Mr Ku pointed to him and said to Ongnyŏn that a Chinese like that would certainly not be illiterate. He shouted at him frantically, and the man in the coach heard him, but the horse which was pulling the coach could not have heard him, since it just galloped on. The coach went out of range of Mr Ku's voice, so the Chinese in it told the coachman to stop, jumped out lightly, and went over to Mr Ku. Mr Ku started to write something with a pencil, but when the Chinese saw that Ongnyŏn was wearing Japanese clothes, he thought that she was Japanese, and he turned to her and asked her something in Japanese. Ongnyŏn was overcome with happiness, and went over to him and spoke to him in reply. Mr Ku stopped writing and just stood there. Actually the Chinese had only been on a short trip to Japan, and although he understood one or two words of Japanese, he could not keep up a long conversation. As Ongnyŏn's words streamed out, he gradually lost the sense of what she was saying. All he could understand was that she was saying that they were Koreans. So he turned to Mr Ku again, and got the outline of the story from him in writing. He took out his card, wrote a few words on it by way of request to a friend, and gave it to them. They saw that it was the card of the famous K'ang Yu-wei of the Chinese Reform Party. The man they took the card to was a Chinese who both spoke Japanese well and had been in San Francisco for many years. He was good enough to arrange for Mr Ku and Ongnyŏn to go to Washington.

Episode Thirty-Seven (Thursday, September 20, 1906)

They went to school and studied with the Chinese students. For five years in Washington in America Ongnyŏn never missed a day at school, and she was so clever and diligent in her work that she was praised as the best girl in the school. In the final examination she was top of the high school, and so her name and her school record were mentioned in a Washington paper.

One man read the report with particular happiness. He was so happy that he could not help bursting into tears. He was overcome with happiness, but then he began to have his doubts and muttered to himself.

'That's the story of a Korean written in English, and it may not have been properly transcribed. It's ten years since I came to America, but I am still confused in English, and I may not have read it properly'

The name of the man who was being so overcautious was Kim Kwanil, and his daughter's name was Ongnyŏn. When the Sino-Japanese War had broken out, he had not known whether his daughter had survived it or not, and he had come to America. Now the Washington paper had a short article giving Ongnyŏn's school record, and saying that she was from

P'yŏngyang, and had gone to Ōsaka at the age of seven, gone through a Common Elementary School there, and then had come to Washington and finished at high school. Mr Kim could not say for sure that it was his daughter, but it said that her name was Ongnyŏn, that she was from P'yŏngyang, and that she had left home at the age of seven, and Mr Kim could not help feeling positive in his own mind that it was his daughter. So he called at the school, but at that time the school was having its summer holidays after the school-leaving ceremony for the students. Since there was no one at the school, and nowhere to make enquiries, Mr Kim went away again without having been able to meet Ongnyŏn.

Episode Thirty-Eight (Friday, September 21, 1906)

On the day she left school, Ongnyŏn returned to her hotel carrying her certificate. As the proprietor congratulated her, he noticed that she had a strange expression on her face. Ongnyŏn looked as if she had all the cares of the world on her shoulders, and she took no dinner, but just gazed at the sun going down towards the hills in the west and sighed.

Just then she was told that there was a visitor outside to see her, and when she took the card and looked at it, her face lit up again. She told the boy to show the visitor in, and when he followed the boy in, Ongnyŏn jumped up happily and welcomed him with a handshake. They sat on chairs facing each other across a table. Her visitor was the young man who had travelled with her from Ōsaka in Japan, Wu Wansŏ.

'Congratulations on finishing school! Ah, women are cleverer than men. A year after you came to America, you could understand what people were talking about in English. You even went to school, and now this year you've finished, but it took me two years after coming to America to get into middle school, and I'll only finish next year. All I can do is raise the white flag and surrender to you!'

Ongnyŏn had grown up in Japan as a little girl, and so she used a lot of Japanese expressions in her reply.

'It is by your gracious favour that I have been able to study as I have, and I am deeply grateful.'

She was steeped in Japanese customs, which was why she

spoke the way she did, but Mr Ku had been brought up in Korea. Ongnyŏn was a child, and he had used to her the form of speech one uses to a child in the Korean custom. But, he thought, he was a child too.

'Now, come on, if we are Koreans, let's chat in the Korean way. When we first met, you were only a little girl, so I spoke to you as I do to children, but now you're sixteen, and so big that I feel awkward talking to you as if you were a child.'

'If you say "let's speak in the Korean way", how can you feel awkward speaking to a child as if she were a child?'

This sent Mr Ku into fits of laughter.

'I'm a child too. I'm still not married. We're both equally children. You should speak to me as if I were a child too, so just do that, and don't make a fuss. Then I won't feel uneasy at speaking to you as if you were a child.'

Episode Thirty-Nine (Saturday, September 22, 1906)

'I thought you had a wife. You said you were seventeen when you came to America. How is it that you hadn't married, when it's the custom to marry early in countries like Korea?'

Mr Ku laughed: 'You're still not speaking to me as a child, so I'll use polite speech back to you. But I haven't answered your question. I'm very sorry. When I was in Korea, my parents tried to get me to marry in my early teens, but I said no, Korean child marriages are not right. After I've been to college and have enough education and knowledge, however long it takes, I'll look for a woman who is also educated for a wife, and marry her. If you marry someone with no education or knowledge, someone who just gets more and more babyish in her speech, it's just like animals mating. You know nothing but the physical pleasures of marriage. That is why we Koreans are like animals, thinking only of our own bodies and our own wives and children. We never think of doing anything for our country. In fact we are robbers and devourers of our country's wealth. We are so mad that we go about turning everything upside down. And it's all because we get no education when we're young. People like us, who've been born in a civilised world, and come so far from home to learn to be useful to our country, and to undertake work which will be a credit to our society, must keep grinding away at our studies. Every day I'm getting more and better education, such as they have in foreign countries, and more and better knowledge, such as they have in foreign countries. To get married now, and to waste all my energies on sexual pleasures is not the way of a man with ambitions as great as mine. I'm right, aren't I, Ongnyŏn?'

The vigour of every word that Mr Ku spoke swept away Ongnyŏn's cares. She laughed as she said,

'When I hear you arguing like that, I feel better. Oh, but when I'm alone, then . . .'

She broke off and gazed at Mr Ku. He could tell at a glance what was on her mind, but he was not the sort of man to waste time or energy. He took out his watch, looked at it, jumped up, and said good-bye. Ongnyŏn listened to his footsteps as he went down, and returned to sitting on the chair and looking at the far-off hill. All the cares she had had before returned. She gave a sigh, there by herself.

Episode Forty (Sunday, September 23, 1906)

She went through all her life. She thought of the past and worried about the future. She felt very unsettled.

'How quickly time passed. It seems only yesterday that I came to America from Japan. When I was in Ōsaka in Japan, on the day I finished at the Common Elementary School I tried to kill myself twice in one night. Today I can't help wondering again whether the stars are against me or something. It wasn't because I didn't want to die that I didn't kill myself, and it wasn't because I wanted to study that I came here. When I had made up my mind to kill myself at Ōsaka harbour, and tried to throw myself into the water, my heart was full of bitterness. Perhaps that was why, when my mother told me in my dreams not to kill myself, although they were only dreams, they were as vivid as real life. So she soothed my sadness and my life was saved. But there was nowhere in the whole wide world for me to hide myself. I set out aimlessly for Tōkyō, and on the train, by the mercy of heaven, I met a fellow-countryman. At every step in my life up to today I have owed my life to someone else. I can't expect to depend on others for ever, but if I said that I didn't want anyone else's help, I couldn't keep myself even for one day. What am I to do? If I knew that my parents were alive, I wouldn't mind depending on others to keep me, but I don't know whether they're alive or dead, and what use will it be for me to go on living all alone? It would have been better if I'd killed myself in Ōsaka. At least I wouldn't have known these cares. Why was my life saved? If life is nothing but this sort of anxiety, the best thing is to die and escape it all. But even if I wanted to kill myself here and now, I couldn't do it. Mr Ku would think it very wrong of me. I've had every kindness from him, and if I killed myself without repaying him, it would be base ingratitude. What shall I do?'

She brooded on, sitting on the chair through the night until she passed out.

(The newspaper was not published the following day, a Monday, and the issue of Tuesday, September 25, carried no episode.)

Episode Forty-One (Wednesday, September 26, 1906)

She fell asleep and dreamt that it was the Autumn Moon Festival in P'yŏngyang, the high feast of the year. P'yŏngyang was swarming with people. The children were dressed in their new holiday clothes, eating toffee and fruit until they burst, and gasping for breath as they ran all over the place. The grown-ups had had so much to drink that they had lost all sense of reality. They were so blind drunk that they bumped into each other as they passed each other. The falsetto singing of ballads, like the voices of nightingales, mixed with the sweet voices of the harps. In every house in every street the sound could be heard.

So the walled city was full of gaiety, but Ongnyŏn in her dream felt nothing of the gaiety as she made her way with a heavy heart to the hillside graves of her parents. She left by the North Gate, and went up Peony Peak. There was a double grave, as big as a Koryŏ tomb. Ongnyŏn went and sat down before the mound and took two apples from her pouch.

'Here, mother, look at these big apples. I bought them for

you as I left America. Give one to father, and have one yourself.'

She placed one in front of each mound, and suddenly the twin tombs disappeared, and the two corpses sat up and ate the apples. Their flesh had rotted away, and the corpses were nothing but haggard bones. As they ate the apples all their teeth fell out, and lay in front of them like gourd seeds spread out to dry. Ongnyŏn was filled with terror, and screamed in her nightmare.

Day had dawned and it had long been light. The girl in the next room had got up and was on her way down to the lavatory when, as she was passing Ongnyŏn's door, she heard her scream in her nightmare. She could not go uninvited into somebody else's room, but she panicked, and rang the bell urgently. When the boy came, she told him that there had been a most strange cry from Ongnyŏn's room. As the boy opened Ongnyŏn's door, the noise of the door woke her, and she realised that it had only been a dream.

Episode Forty-Two (Thursday, September 27, 1906)

As she awoke from her terrifying dream, she felt relieved, but when she thought back to it, sadness overcame her, and she brooded to herself out loud, unconsciously.

'What are dreams? Should one believe them? If I do, last night's dream means that my parents are not alive. Should one not believe them? If I don't, it was futile to think that my parents were alive after I had those dreams at Ōsaka. Whether dreams are true or not, it means unhappiness for me. But then, come to think of it, the dream was all futile. My father died in the war, so even if he had any relatives, they could not have found his body. And there were only the three of us in our family, and the only one who survived was me, the seven year old unfaithful daughter, Ongnyŏn. Who was there to find my father's body? The crows which flap in the dusk over Peony Peak tore the entrails out of the bodies of the war dead and hung them on the high branches of old trees. Who is there in the world who would be so kind as to find my father's body and give it a proper burial in a grave as magnificent as a Koryŏ tomb?

'And my mother went to kill herself by throwing herself in the waters of the Taedong River. She wrote her farewell to the world on the wall. The interpreter from the field hospital at P'yŏngyang wept as he read it, and it seems like only yesterday when I remember how he told me what it said. When I had my dreams at Ōsaka harbour, I thought that my mother might be alive, but it was a silly thought. My mother certainly drowned herself. She must have become food for the fishes in the flowing waters of the Taedong River, so how can she have had a proper burial like that on Peony Peak?'
(The newspaper of Friday, September 28, carried no episode.)

Episode Forty-Three (Saturday, September 29, 1906)

Ongnyŏn determined to put out of her mind all thoughts of her parents, and made up her mind to accept life as it came to her. She pulled herself together, took out the books she had been studying, and set her mind to them. After two or three days, she found an interest in them again.

One day the boy came to her room with a newspaper. He spread it out in front of her, and pointed to an advertisement in it. Ongnyŏn was astonished as she read it. Her eyes filled with tears and her face turned red as she half cried and half laughed. It made her so happy that she could not read it right to the end. She sat staring blankly. Then she took another look at it, and began to doubt it.

'The other day I went to Peony Peak, to the hillside graves of my parents. Was that a dream, or is it a dream now that I am reading the advertisement in today's paper?'

She read it once in English and once in Korean, and finally translated it into proper written Korean with Chinese characters. It read:

> 'Notice.
> 'There was a report in the gossip columns of the popular press on the thirteenth last that a Korean girl, Kim Ongnyŏn, was top of a certain school, and the advertiser wishes to know the hotel where she is staying. Anyone telling the advertiser the hotel where Ongnyŏn is staying is offered a suitable reward of ten dollars.

'Kim Kwanil, of P'yŏngyang, P'yŏngan Province, Korea.
'Present address . . .'

There could be no doubt that it was her father who had inserted the advertisement.

'If you go with me, with this paper, my father will give you ten dollars reward, so let's go at once.'

'I have done nothing to earn a reward, miss, and I don't want one, but if I went with you and saw how happy you are when you meet, I'd be glad to do so, out of friendship for a young lady we've had here for many years.'

This made Ongnyŏn even happier, and she took him along.

Episode Forty-Four (Sunday, September 30, 1906)

They went to look for where her father was.

Ongnyŏn thought they had both changed in the ten years that had passed, and they might not recognize each other at sight. She took the advertisement and her card to her father, and introduced herself to him very formally, as if she had never met him before. However, once they were sure of each other, Ongnyŏn felt again as babyish as she had been at the age of seven. She sat on his knee with her head down and wept silently. Kim Kwanil's tears fell onto the back of her head, and her tears soaked her father's knees.

'All right, Ongnyŏn, now get up and have a look at your mother's letters.'

'Mother's letters? Is mother alive?'

She looked up, as surprised as if the world had come to an end. Her father wiped away her tears with his handkerchief, without a thought of wiping way his own tears, and Ongnyŏn had turned into such a baby again that she put up her face for him to wipe them away.

Kim Kwanil opened a case, took out a bundle of letters, and, flicking through them, took out one and gave it to Ongnyŏn.

'Here, read this carefully. This is the first one that came.'

Ongnyŏn took the letter and looked at it, but she did not know her mother's writing. If she had tried hard, she might perhaps have remembered her mother's face, but since she had left her mother at the age of seven, when she did not even know the alphabet, she said now, as she read the letter,

'I don't even know my mother's writing. Is this what it's like?'

She spread out the letter in front of her father and read:

'Dear husband,

It is less than three months since you left, but when you were here in P'yŏngyang seems as if it were another life. I have been worried no end that something awful might have happened to you, and wondering whether you are in good health. I will not bore you will all the details of what I have been through, but will just give you a brief outline so that you will know the news. I thought Ongnyŏn must have died, anyway, I had no news of her, and so I determined to kill myself and threw myself into the waters of the Taedong River. However, I was fished out by a boatman and Ko Changp'al, and my life was saved. My father came from Pusan, and told me that you had gone to America, and since then I have been fully occupied with looking after myself. I am just waiting for the time to pass quickly and for you to come back home as you promised. But even if you do not come back for many years, it is a consolation that you are alive. Only I do not think that I shall see Ongnyŏn again before I go to the grave, and that is a great sorrow.

'I could go on for ever, but will stop there.'

Ongnyŏn read the letter, and . . .

(The newspaper was not published the next day, a Monday, and the next episode was again numbered 44.)

Episode Forty-Four (Tuesday, October 2, 1906)

She sat quietly, feeling as if her bones were turning to jelly, and her body was melting away.

'Father, send me home, tomorrow if possible. I would like to grow wings and fly there now, this very minute, so that I could see my mother's face and free her of her sorrow.'

'There's not all that much hurry for you to go home. First

tell me all you've been through. How did you survive, and how did you get here?'

Ongnyŏn told every detail of her story, without showing any emotion, and sitting up straight: how she had been wounded on Peony Peak and gone to the field hospital; how she had gone to Major Inoue's house; how she had left Ōsaka because of her unhappiness; and how she had found a happy ending to her troubles by meeting Ku Wansŏ on the train to Tōkyō. When she finished, her expression changed again, and tears rolled down. But her tears were nothing to do with her feeling for her parents, nor were they from thinking of her own fate. She wept as she thought of the kindness of Ku Wansŏ.

'Father, if you're happy to have found such a bad daughter as me again, you should find Mr Ku and thank him.'

Kim Kwanil agreed, and took Ongnyŏn straightaway to call on Mr Ku where he was staying. When Mr Ku met Kim Kwanil, he felt as thankful as if he were meeting his own father, not meeting Ongnyŏn's father. This was because he felt exactly as if Ongnyŏn's happiness were his happiness. Mr Kim was as thankful to meet Mr Ku as he had been to meet his daughter again. That was how the two men felt. Mr Kim said only two simple things to Mr Ku. First he thanked him for all that Ongnyŏn owed him, and then he said that he wished that after Mr Ku returned home he would take Ongnyŏn for better or for worse and tie the eternal knot.

Now Mr Ku was a vigorous man, who talked straight.

(The newspaper was not published the following day, Wednesday, October 3.)

Episode Forty-Five (Thursday, October 4, 1906)

He looked steadily at Ongnyŏn.

'Ongnyŏn — oh, how rude of me, addressing another man's daughter by her personal name like that! We may speak in Korean, but our hearts are steeped in the civilised customs of the west. If we do get married, it would be as westerners do, not at the command of our parents. If we two are thinking of becoming man and wife, the right thing is for us to talk directly to each other. But let's make a start by talking in English. If we talk in Korean, we have this habit of my talking to you as if you were a child, which makes me feel awkward.'

So Mr Ku talked to Ongnyŏn in English. He was much more highly educated than Ongnyŏn, but in English Ongnyŏn was almost good enough to be his teacher. But while Mr Ku talked in his untidy English, Ongnyŏn replied neatly and tidily in Korean.

Kim Kwanil had proposed his daughter's marriage, but when Mr Ku insisted that he and Ongnyŏn should talk it over directly together in the western way, Mr Kim sat quiet, having no right to make any decisions on his daughter's marriage contract.

Ongnyŏn, for all that she was a Korean girl, was educated and enlightened in her thinking, and had seen a lot of the world. So she answered without hesitation in this discussion of their marriage. Mr Ku asked one thing, that he and Ongnyŏn should continue studying hard for several more years until they had all the education they wanted, before they went home and got married. Then Ongnyŏn could take upon herself the education of Korean women. What he asked showed his ambitions, and when Ongnyŏn heard what he proposed, she firmly made up her mind to educate Korean women, and contracted to marry Mr Ku.

The purpose in Mr Ku's mind was like Bismarck's, to study hard, and, after returning home, to make a federation of Korea like Germany, and by joining it with Japan and Manchuria to create a civilised great power. Ongnyŏn wanted to study hard, and, after returning home, to broaden the knowledge of Korean women and help them to get equal rights with men, instead of being oppressed by men, and then to educate them so that the women too would become useful citizens in the land and honoured persons in society.

Episode Forty-Six (Friday, October 5, 1906)

There is nothing in the world so enjoyable as determining one's own aims oneself. Ku Wansŏ and Ongnyŏn had gone abroad while they were young. They did not know that Koreans were so barbarous and so stupidly selfish. They both thought that when the day came for them to return to Korea there would be many ambitious people in Korea too who would listen to the words of educated and knowledgeable people, and approve of them, so that everything would turn out as Mr Ku planned, and that, as Ongnyŏn planned, the women of Korea would all get her training, and that everywhere many people would arise with an education like hers. Their happiness knew no bounds, but they did not know the situation in their country, and their feelings were the product of the hopefulness of youthful students who had studied abroad.

But whether things turned out as Mr Ku and Ongnyŏn planned or not was a matter of the future. On that day even their happiness at contracting marriage took second place in their hearts. It was the first time Ongnyŏn had known such happiness since her birth.

When Kim Kwanil met Ongnyŏn, he accepted Ku Wansŏ as his son-in-law. When he heard that Mr Ku and Ongnyŏn had such wonderful aims, his happiness too knew no bounds.

While Ongnyŏn and her father and Mr Ku made such a happy group sitting in a hotel in Washington in America, it was not like that everywhere in the world. In Korea, inside the North Gate of P'yŏngyang, in a low, crab-shell of a house, there was a lady, without a husband before she was thirty, with no children of her own flesh and blood, living without means. For ten years there was one thing she had had more of then anybody else, and that was anxiety.

Was her husband dead, that she had lost him, you may ask? No, he was not dead. If he were, she would have given up thinking of him, but he had gone sixty thousand leagues away, and she was as miserable a thing as a memorial stone to a dead husband.

Had she not been able to give birth, that she was without children of her own flesh and blood, you might ask? She had had one daughter, who had been both son and daughter to her, and she had cherished her as gold or jewels, but she had lost her in her seventh year. If you asked whether she had seen her child's untimely death with her own eyes, she would just weep silently. If she had died before her eyes, where she could see her, she would have felt no sorrow or anything, but she did not know where she had died, and that was her sorrow.

Episode Forty-Seven (Saturday, October 6, 1906)

She had folded up carefully one garment that her daughter had worn, put it in a hand-box which her daughter had owned, and written on the box in her own handwriting 'This is the casket of Ongnyŏn'. She had buried it on the slope of Peony Peak. On festivals such as Cold Food Day or the Autumn Moon Festival she would go there and weep, and then return home.

Now it happened just to be the day of the full harvest moon, and Mrs Kim called Ko Changp'al's mother.

'Here, Granny, today must be the Autumn Moon Festival. Won't you go with me to our Ongnyŏn's tomb? How time flies! It's nine years now since Ongnyŏn died and my husband went to America. America may be a long way away, but at least my husband is alive and I will see him again, but Ongnyŏn, she's dead and gone for ever, and . . .'

Her voice trailed way and choked in her throat. She sat silently. Every day since the Sino-Japanese War she had passed in anxiety and weeping. Perhaps even her eyes had changed, anyway, now, however sad her thoughts were, no tears came. There was only the pain in her breast.

She seemed to see Ongnyŏn before her eyes, and seemed to hear Ongnyŏn's voice in her ears. If she thought of her, she seemed to be demented. When she had such thoughts, no food entered her mouth, no sleep came to her eyes, all her movements were sluggish, and she hated even to walk.

Ko Changp'al's mother went and bought some unripe chestnuts, jujubes and pears, and brought them home and placed them in front of Mrs Kim.

'Mistress, I've brought the fruit. Let's go to baby Ongnyŏn's tomb. Mistress! Mistress! Mistress! Mistress!'

Whether Mrs Kim heard her calling her or not, she sat quietly, like a living Buddha. Ko Changp'al's mother gazed at Mrs Kim's face, and with tears streaming down her cheeks said,

'Oh dear, mistress, are you feeling like that again? Mistress, mistress, what's the use of thinking of the dead baby Ongnyŏn like that? Come on, think of something else! My goodness, the King of Hell must be heartless. If I were him I'd return the baby Ongnyŏn to life, and send her back to this world, to console the heart of my mistress, which is filled with bitter sorrow.

'Mistress, when you think of the baby Ongnyŏn like that, how pleased you would be if Ongnyŏn came back to life and came toddling into this courtyard. Oh, if only I could see such a thing!'

Episode Forty-Eight (Sunday, October 7, 1906)

Just then a crow settled on the roof, and cawed in such a wicked way that Mrs Kim, who had had her eyes closed, opened them and called to Changp'al's mother.

'Just listen to the noise that crow's making! It looks as if there's going to be more trouble. They say a crow is a bird of omen. Perhaps something else is going to happen. Fate's been against me for long enough, and I'd rather die today than go through any more. And there's been no letter from America lately. I wonder why?'

Anyone could have seen that she was unhappy as she moaned to herself in a voice that had no strength, and dear old Mrs Ko, as she looked at Mrs Kim, felt that if her mistress died, she would follow her to death. She also felt that she wanted to strike that crow dead, and, flouncing down into the courtyard, she looked up at the roof and pretended to throw things at the crow. She swore at it.

'Shoo! I'll give it to you, you rascal! Where've all the men with the guns gone? You bastard son of a salt-merchant!'

She hurled every Korean epithet at the crow. Changp'al's mother knew them all, and screamed every one of them at him. The crow leapt up and flew high into the air, cawing, over towards Peony Peak. Mrs Kim's eyes followed him over to the peak, and Mrs Ko's shouts of abuse went away after his cawing.

'A letter for you! A letter for you!' a voice cried two or three times. It was the postman peeping through the inner gate, with his postman's hat, his tight black suit, and a leather satchel over his shoulder. Changp'al's mother was still bursting with rage at the crow, and she did not listen carefully who this might be, or exactly what he was saying, but laid into the postman furiously for no reason at all, with a voice like two rough bits of pottery grating against each other.

'Who d'you think you are, peeping without so much as a by-your-leave into the inner court of someone's house? The master's not even here. What sort of a fellow are you, peeping into the inner court of a gentleman's residence?'

'Who are you calling fellow? D'you think a postman's nothing at all? Let me get a word in! Come out here! The only thing I've done wrong is to try and deliver a letter.'

(The newspaper was not published the following day, a Monday.)

Episode Forty-Nine (Tuesday, October 9, 1906)

'Granny, who're you squabbling with? The postman said he's brought a letter, and it looks as if it's from America, from my husband. Take it off him and bring it in to me.'

'Oh, it's the postman! My old eyes are so dim. Give me the letter, please, and I'll take it to my mistress.'

When the old woman had first screamed at him, the postman had thought that it was some old crone in her dotage, and had spoken reasonably politely, but when he saw that the old woman realized that she had done something wrong and was apologizing then he retorted, shrieking as if his throat were being cut.

'You ——! This is the first time I've had anything like this on my rounds as a postman. What are you swearing at me for? I've got my work to do, but I'm not leaving here until you answer me that.'

He screamed back at her, and took no notice of her asking for the letter. P'yŏngyang people get so mad when they quarrel that they will not let up, even if it kills them on the spot. If the old woman had still been as furious as she had been with the crow, she would have set about the postman, and all her fury would not have evaporated, even if it killed her, but when she heard 'a letter from America', her fury evaporated. Not only that, but she even took the postman's rudeness. Mrs Kim was so keen to see the letter that she seemed to have no sense of decorum as she ran out to the inner gate. She scolded the old woman, and calmed the postman down, offering him the wine and fruit which she had been taking to Ongnyŏn's grave.

The postman had been ready to do murder, but he calmed down, calling the old woman 'grandmother', as nicely as if he were a servant in the house. Mrs Ko took the letter to Mrs Kim, but when Mrs Kim took it and saw what was written on the envelope, she was surprised and puzzled.

'What's the matter, mistress?'

'Wait a minute!'

'Is it a letter from the master?'

'I don't think so.'

'Well, is it a letter from Pusan, from your father?'

'No.'

'For heaven's sake tell me, and put me out of my agony!'

'I've never seen the writing before.'

Episode Fifty (Wednesday, October 10, 1906)

Of course, Ongnyŏn had left her parents when she was seven, and at that time she had not known a single letter of the alphabet. Later she had gone to Japan, and had got as far as finishing the Common Elementary School without having even a sight of the Korean alphabet. After that, while she was crossing the Pacific to America with Ku Wansŏ, he had taught her the alphabet. So how could her mother recognize Ongnyŏn's writing? She looked at it, and on the front it said:

To the wife of Kim Kwanil,
Inside the North Gate, P'yŏngyang,
South P'yŏngan Province, Korea

On the other side it said:

From Ongnyŏn, ... Hotel,
Washington, U.S.A.

Mrs Kim could not read a single Chinese character, and all she could read was 'from Ongnyŏn'. She did not know whose writing it was, and the more she looked at the name 'Ongnyŏn', the more puzzled she was.

'Here, Mrs Ko, has the postman who brought this letter gone? We should have asked him whether he was sure that this letter was for here.'

'Why, doesn't it say so?'

'There are Chinese characters on one side, and on the other side Chinese characters and Korean writing. I don't know what the Chinese characters are, and the Korean says "from Ongnyŏn". It's very strange. Can there be anyone else in the world called Ongnyŏn? Even if there were, there is none with any reason to send me a letter.'

'Well then, it looks as if it must be from the young mistress.'

'It sounds like a dream. A letter from Ongnyŏn, who's dead. How . . .'

She sighed, and the sadness came over her face again.

'Mistress, don't waste words. Open the letter.'

Mrs Kim tore the letter open excitedly, the letter from Ongnyŏn. It told all her story in every graphic detail, from the night she had spent on Peony Peak to her meeting her father in a Washington hotel and reading her mother's letters.

The letter had been posted on the eleventh day of the seventh month by the lunar calender in the sixth year of Kwangmu (that is, August 14, 1902), and the day Mrs Kim received it was the fifteenth day of the eighth month by the lunar calender in the Year of the Black Tiger (September 9, 1902).

The reader may look forward to the return of the girl to her homeland in the sequel.

translated by W.E. Skillend

End of Volume 1.

Postscript:

Yi Injik began to serialize the sequel, under the title of 'Peony Peak', in the *Mail Sinbo* in 1913, but it never really took shape, and he abandoned it after a few episodes.

'Tears of Blood' was printed as a book in 1907 and 1908, with some deliberate amendations, but also some serious misprints, including the omission of the whole of Episode 47.

Pirate reprints may have been made during the Japanese occupation, and certainly were current immediately after liberation, with the story still discernible, and the message as in 1906 still clear, but with the text so corrupted as to take all literary merit from the work. Meanwhile, in 1940, a complete rewriting of the work was published in the literary magazine *Munjang*. This meticulously removed every patriotic phrase, even every use of the word 'country' for Korea, and thereby reduced all the male characters in the work to feckless, ineffectual caricatures. Professor Chŏn Kwangyong began the restoration of Yi Injik's reputation in 1957, and, although he was certainly not the greatest writer that Korea has ever produced, we hope that this presentation of his work, as it was first published, will have indicated the nature of the impact which he had on the course of Korean prose fiction.

For Product Safety Concerns and Information please contact our EU representative GPSR@taylorandfrancis.com
Taylor & Francis Verlag GmbH, Kaufingerstraße 24, 80331 München, Germany

www.ingramcontent.com/pod-product-compliance
Lightning Source LLC
Chambersburg PA
CBHW071528110726
47908CB00003B/989

* 9 7 8 1 1 3 8 9 7 4 0 9 8 *